A Different Shade of Blue:

How Women Changed the Face of Police Work

by
Adam Eisenberg

Behler™
PUBLICATIONS
California
USA

Behler Publications
California

A Different Shade of Blue
A Behler Publications Book

Copyright © 2009 by Adam Eisenberg
Cover design by Cathy Scott – www.mbcdesigns.com

A version of "Chapter Five: The First Nine" appeared in *The Seattle Post-Intelligencer,* and online at *HistoryLink.org.* © 2001 by Adam Eisenberg.

Photos courtesy of:
Seattle Police Department
Cameron Covington
Lis Eddy
Joanne Hunt
Helen Karas
Photo of Suzanne Parton by Sean Jordan, SPD Photo Unit
Photo of Lis Eddy, 2008, by Alex Worden, SPD Photo Unit
Photo of Dalgit Gill by Matt Vielbig
Backcover photo of author by Paul Verba
All photos used with permission.

Eisenberg, Adam.
    A different shade of blue : how women changed the face of police work / by Adam Eisenberg.
    p. cm.
    ISBN-13: 978-1-933016-56-6 (pbk.)
    ISBN-10: 1-933016-56-6
    1. Policewomen--Washington (State)--Seattle--History. 2. Police--Washington (State)--Seattle--History. I. Title.
    HV8023.E57 2009
    363.2082'09797772--dc22
                                    2009007646

FIRST PRINTING

ISBN: 1-933016-56-6
ISBN 13 978-1-933016-56-6
Published by Behler Publications, LLC
Lake Forest, California
www.behlerpublications.com

Manufactured in the United States of America

Throughout my life I have been blessed with the mentorship of many women. To all those who have encouraged and inspired me, I give my sincerest thanks. Among the many, I dedicate this book to:

Mary Harkins Berrong, for your guidance
Marion Kapner, for your eternal optimism
Martha Markowitz, for your generous spirit
and
Ruth Goldin Eisenberg
for your unquestioning love

Table of Contents

Foreword
by Ann Rule

bestselling author of *The Stranger Beside Me,*
Small Sacrifices, and *Mortal Danger*

When I joined the Seattle Police Department in the mid-1950s, the image of a policewoman was in a state of flux. We had representatives of the old, the new, and the in-between working in the Women's Division on the third floor of the Public Safety Building, located on Third Avenue between James and Cherry. It was a new building then, modern, sleek, and it fit the police department's needs perfectly.

The bronze plaque outside the Fourth Avenue entrance read:

"Where there is no justice, the people perish.
But he that keepeth the law, happy is he."

Over the next half-century, I must have read that plaque thousands of times. It has long since been tattooed on my brain.

As the years passed, the Public Safety Building became shopworn, a little dingy and crowded, and, finally, obsolete. There is a new building now a few blocks east, as resplendent today as the one I entered in 1954, when I was full of excitement about my new job, and trepidation about all that it would entail.

The police station where I worked has been reduced to rubble and swept away, and the gap along Third Avenue jars my heart. Today, I have a single chunk of marble from the Public Safety Building in my garden, a reminder of another time and of what, for me, was the culmination of my lifelong ambition — to be a police officer.

A week after I graduated from the University of Washington, I applied to become a Seattle police officer. I was not quite twenty-one and I had so much to learn. Even though I had interned at a girl's training (read *reform*) school in Oregon, worked nights at the Youth Service Center on East Alder where juvenile offenders were housed, and taken every criminology, penology, and psychology course the University of Washington offered, my naiveté was profound. Looking back, it almost embarrasses me to think how little I knew about the world of the good guys and the bad guys.

I was a virgin assigned to taking sexual assault statements, and didn't understand all the terms used, although I got pretty skilled at faking it. I tended to believe people at face value, but I soon learned to look behind the smooth façades of psychopathic liars. I lost the very first "prisoner" I ever transported when I took her to Harborview Hospital and she pretended to feel faint and asked me to find her a bed. I left her alone for about three minutes, and of course she was long gone when I came back for her.

I was lucky not to get fired during my first week on the job for that. Very lucky—because my year or so on the Seattle Police Department was one of the true highpoints of my life. All these years later, I can close my eyes and see all of the policewomen sitting at their desks, many of them dear friends to this day.

The captain and sergeant had their own offices, of course, and the rest of us were scattered around a sprawling room that overlooked Third Avenue. Each of us had a battered desk, a manual typewriter, and a phone. Ironically, I—who would go on to write almost three dozen books—was always behind in writing my follow-up reports. My sergeant chastised me when she found piles of notes in my desk drawers.

The "brass" in the Women's Division were Captain Irene Durham, a small, bird-like woman who was full of energy, and Sergeant Helen Elliott, who had genteel manners, white hair, and reminded me of Eleanor Roosevelt. I was in awe of Captain Durham, and always wary of disappointing Sergeant Elliott.

As Adam Eisenberg details in *A Different Shade of Blue*, there were also policewomen working who had been on the department since the 1920s and 30s. "B.J." Bjornsen, who handled mental cases (220s in Seattle Police parlance), and Fern Wheeler, who was in charge of sex crimes, seemed old to me then, although they were probably only in their fifties or sixties. They were big, broad-shouldered women. B.J., a spinster, had gray braids wound tightly around her head, and wore no make-up; Fern dyed her hair an odd shade of magenta-auburn and wore quite a bit of make-up. While B.J. had her desk in the corner of the Women's Division, Fern worked in the "Morals Division" one floor up.

Yes, that's what they called the unit that handled sexual assaults half a century ago. It always sounded to me as if the victims were somehow being held responsible for the attacks they'd suffered. It wasn't a matter of morals at all; it dealt with crimes of sexually motivated violence and perversion.

Fern Wheeler was tough, and perhaps somewhat jaded. Adrift in an office of male detectives who worked sex crimes and Bunco con games, Fern dominated the room, older than them all, and far more experienced. Nothing seemed to embarrass her.

Kay Twohig was probably in her forties, had very curly red hair, and was descended from other family members in the Seattle Department. Helen Mae Griffith was in the same age group. She was blond, a little plump—as Kay was—but quiet and shy, whereas Kay's voice and manner could be raucous. They had back-to-back desks just outside Captain Durham's spacious office.

Then there were more recent hires: Phyllis Covington, Kay Callender, Helen Karas, Mary Stowe, Norma Alex, Jean Selvidge Dunbar, Pat Mikkelborg, Joyce Montgomery Johnson, and those of us who worked provisionally until the next Civil Service test came around. The new hires were Rosemary Codd, Jane Paulsen, and myself. Every one of us had a unique personality, possibly because it took a woman who walked her own path to want to be a police officer. Later, Noreen Skagen, a college classmate of mine who eventually became Assistant Chief, Beryl Thompson, and Karen Ejde joined the Women's Division.

Phyllis was very tall and very thin, and dressed like a fashion model. She had huge eyes and hollow cheeks that further emphasized her model-like appearance. Her demeanor was always serious. Kay Callender was also very tall, and she struggled with her weight all the time. But she was gorgeous with chestnut hair and snapping brown eyes, and her sense of humor was totally unlike Phyllis's personality.

Mary Stowe, who probably served longer on the department than any of us—and retired not long ago as a lieutenant—had thick golden curls that she caught up in ribbons. Sometimes we called her "Mary Sunshine" because she didn't look like a cop at all back then. Helen Karas, another long-time officer, had thick, wavy dark hair, befitting her Greek heritage, a buxom figure, and a heart of gold—which she tried to hide by being gruff. Helen was one of the best police officers I ever knew, and she was once selected as Master Detective's "Police Officers of the Month." I was honored to write the article that went with her award.

Jean Selvidge Dunbar was petite and slim and extremely efficient. She and I shared a background in journalism. Jean was very "take charge," and thought rapidly on her feet. Pat Mikkelborg had brown hair with a few premature gray strands, and dark eyes. She was always good-natured.

Norma Alex was the only policewoman of the younger group who didn't have a college degree, but she probably knew more than any of us. I know she taught me a lot. When I think of Norma, I think of energy. Norma had red hair then, which she styled like Lucille Ball, and freckles. Oddly, I can't visualize Norma sitting still.

Joyce Montgomery Johnson was my best friend in the Women's Division, and we would remain close until her death in 2003. I still find myself reaching for the phone to call her, and ask her if she remembers something I've forgotten—particularly as I write this foreword. She was always patient with me, and invited me to her apartment often for dinner. Her rent was seventeen dollars a month, and I split an apartment with a college friend for forty dollars a month.

When I joined the force, we were paid three hundred dollars a month, with a twenty-five-dollar raise after six months; I made more than any of my friends.

Joyce was a tall blond Swede from Minnesota, and she signed on to the Seattle Police Department when she was in her twenties. But shortly after, on a whim, she dropped into a tuberculosis screening van parked in front of the old Rhodes Department Store. She was shocked to find that she had the disease. Instead of working as a police officer, she went to the Fir Lands Sanitarium for over a year, lost a lobe of one lung to surgery, and when she was finally released, she doubted that her police career would ever start again.

It did. Joyce managed to pass all the physical tasks of the Civil Service test—even with half a lung missing—and had a long career with the Women's Division. She worked sexual assault cases and sometimes homicides. She was extremely skilled at doing difficult interviews.

After I left the department, I introduced Joyce to a man named Bill Johnson who worked with me at the Washington State Department of Public Assistance.

When I called three days later to see how the blind date had gone, Joyce said, "Pretty well. We went to Coeur D'Alene, Idaho, and got married!"

I thought she was kidding, but she wasn't. Joyce and Bill were married over fifty years when she died. I quit my matchmaking role after their elopement, sure I could never do it so well again. They shared common interests and an odd sense of humor, not to mention a daughter, Jessamyn. The Johnsons kayaked, learned to weave Indian baskets from grasses and reeds, had huge gardens, Yorkshire puppies, and, for some reason, a genuine dental chair in their living room instead of a couch.

Although I was the first provisional officer to make it all the way through the many sections of the Civil Service test—from I.Q. tests to doing fifty sit-ups and running up and down four flights of stairs in the specified time—I washed out at the very end on the eye test. Because I was very near-sighted, I could not see the big "E," or even the wall behind it. The sympathetic nurse who gave the test knew how much it meant to me to be a cop, and she let me go half-way up to the eye chart.

I still couldn't see the big "E." We weren't allowed to wear contact lenses back in those days, and I tried in vain to do eye exercises that would help me see better. The truth was that I just plain couldn't see without my glasses. It wasn't until I turned forty and my eyes began to get far-sighted enough to read the chart that I could have passed. By then, I was too old.

I feel very lucky that I've been able to slip over into writing about police work and criminal personalities, but I will always miss being a police officer, just as I keep the memories my fellow policewomen in my heart.

As *A Different Shade of Blue* explains, most of us were glorified social workers. We didn't do police work as women do today. We didn't carry guns, handcuffs, or wear uniforms—except when we were assigned to parades or the Sea Fair hydroplane races. We had badges, keys to the call-boxes, and passes that allowed us to ride free on transit buses. When I see today's women who are *real* cops, wearing uniforms with slacks, bullet-proof vests, and sensible shoes they can run in, I wonder that more of us didn't get hurt.

We wore tight skirts or dresses, three or four-inch heels, and looked more like we were going to afternoon tea than heading for an arrest or to chase someone down.

If we expected a physical skirmish, we usually called for a male car to stand by to bail us out.

Seattle's policewomen of the fifties were mainly called upon to investigate "injurious living conditions" for children, take statements from victims of sexual abuse, try to find runaway girls, and to accompany male officers when they picked up females who were mentally disturbed. Sometimes, we were decoys for con-artist investigations.

I worked undercover a lot at first because I had a fresh face that the Gypsy fortunetellers didn't recognize. It was a violation of the vagrancy code to predict the future for money. That in itself wasn't so bad, but it usually progressed to their replacing real bills with strips of newspaper or charging a vulnerable client a lot of money to ward off danger and death. I remember the day that I had to arrest a Gypsy mother with six little children, all of whom had measles. None of the other policewomen would help me transport them because they had children, and didn't want to carry the measles germs home. Somehow I managed to get all of the wailing youngsters to Harborview Hospital.

Fortunately, I'd already had the measles.

Some police work just broke my heart. Working the night shift, Jean Dunbar and I once spotted a sailor and a crippled, very pregnant, young woman entering a downtown hotel that rented rooms by the half-hour. We followed, and when the manager opened the door to their room, their liaison was already over and the woman was sitting in bed, eating a hamburger, obviously her price for her services. I didn't want to arrest her, but it was the law.

Back at the Public Safety Building, my fiancé was waiting to give me a ride home. He looked at our sad prisoner, and turned away quickly. "Ann," he said quietly, "I went to high school with her. I don't want her to see me and be embarrassed."

I was all for arresting the "Johns" too, but it wasn't done then. They walked off scot-free.

Those of us who worked as provisional officers were sometimes treated like rookies in the army, and usually we didn't argue with the women who had been there years longer than we had. We were there to learn. One of the policewomen with years on the job routinely insisted on driving the police car we'd been assigned. She would never let me answer the radio when our numbers—77 and 78—were broadcast, even though we were in heavy traffic and it was raining buckets. I was completely capable of pressing the button and saying "77 by," but she didn't trust me to do *anything*.

It frustrated me, but I didn't argue with her. Sometimes, though, I stood my ground. One cold night, I got a phone call in the office from a woman I'd dealt with earlier. She was obviously intoxicated, and she said that she, her husband, and her baby were in a Skid Road hotel and she was afraid she would pass out. She wanted me to come get her baby before it got hurt. The senior officer with me said they couldn't possibly be there because the hotel was closed down—out of business. I insisted that we at least go there, and check.

We found one room occupied. They all lay in one bed, its tangled sheets soaked in beer, and dotted with greasy french-fries.

The couple, passed out, was lying on top of the baby, and he was on the verge of suffocating. I picked him up and cuddled him against my neck. Like many of the little children we "rescued," he had lice. For some reason, I never got them.

And there was a five-year-old named Danny who suffered a concussion in a day-care situation. In the hospital, we saw that his heels were blistered because his shoes were much too small. Danny's mother was supposed to be out on Puget Sound fishing. We left messages all over for her, even on ship-to-shore radio, but she never called back. I looked at that little boy with the big brown eyes and wanted so much to take him home with me, but that wasn't possible. I've thought about him often over the years, and prayed he was okay.

If we weren't often called upon to assist in homicide investigations back then, we still saved lives and tried to soften the tragedies many people suffered. Years later, when a female detective was first assigned to the Homicide Unit, the men working there painted her desk bright pink, and teased her unmercifully.

It wasn't going to be an easy transition, even though it made sense to have women working patrol and moving up through the ranks. Women are natural multi-taskers, and we are far more curious about the whys of human behavior than most males are, and can be subtle and successful interrogators. Men have bigger muscles, but female officers have proved they have skills of their own. Men and women in police work complement each other, rather than take anything away.

Even though my near-sightedness meant I couldn't be a cop, I've never really left the Seattle Police Department. Every year, I present the "Ann Rule Award for the Best Written Domestic Violence Report" by a Seattle Police Officer, and many times the winners are female officers, as was true in 2008. I looked at the winner, who was accompanied by her husband, also a Seattle cop, and their two toddlers who had come to watch Mama get her award, and marveled at the changes that have taken place.

As they neared retirement, I knew the women who had joined the Seattle Police Department back in the 1920s. They looked like the solidly built, no-nonsense police "matrons" pictured in the early days of magazines like *True Detective* long before I became one of the chain's reporters, but I don't think they were ever called upon to chase down a thief, arrest a murderer, or engage in hand-to-hand combat. Today's female cops tend to be slender and in good shape, with a solid education in Criminal Justice. Part street cop or patrol officer, part social-worker still, and rising through the ranks past the glass ceiling and the prejudice of a few decades ago.

As *A Different Shade of Blue* chronicles, it is, indeed, a new era.

- Ann Rule

PREFACE

When Lis Eddy joined the Seattle Police Department in 1981, female officers were still a novelty. Many of her male coworkers were less than welcoming, and her first sergeant was downright hostile. At their initial meeting, he took one look at her short, squat, 5'1" frame and bluntly declared: "You're a woman and you're too small. You have no business being on the police department. I'm not sure how you got hired, but I'll do everything I can to see you get fired."

True to his words, the sergeant criticized her every action and repeatedly gave her abysmally low performance evaluations. Eddy's future looked bleak until some of her male coworkers and her captain recognized her value and helped her transfer to a more supportive squad leader. However, despite this positive recognition, the sergeant's words were not easily forgotten. Was she too small? Did she belong in police work? Would her male fellow officers ever truly accept her?

Her day of reckoning came one year later when Eddy suddenly found herself in a deadly struggle for her life.

The incident began innocently enough. An "officer in pursuit" call came in over the radio just as most of the department was changing shifts. As one of the few officers available to respond, Eddy drove to the reporting officer's last known location down by the Duwamish River in Seattle. She found his patrol car and another vehicle stopped in the middle of the street. The driver's door of the patrol car was open but no one was in sight.

Eddy drove slowly past the abandoned cars and turned into a nearby shipping container yard. She soon spotted three men walking their dogs along the river's edge. None of the men fit the suspect's reported description—a man in his mid-thirties wearing a red sweater—but Eddy approached them hoping they might know something.

"As I did so, one of the men started to jog away from the other men, and a dog ran with him," she explains. "My first thought was that he was doing a dog-training. Then the two guys who stayed behind pointed in his general direction and I thought either the jogger was going to lead me to the suspect or he had some information about him."

Eddy followed the jogger down along the riverbank. The man was moving slowly away, but he kept glancing over his shoulder in her direction. When she got close enough, she rolled down her window and called to the man to get his attention.

"He stopped, turned, and started walking toward my car," she recalls. "At that point, I violated a basic officer safety rule because I started to open the car door with one hand while picking up the radio with the other to report in. As I started to speak into the radio, the guy walked up to my window, lifted his sweater, and pulled out a gun. He pointed it at my face and said, 'Don't move.'

"And I didn't. I sat there with the microphone in my hand. Then he told me to slide over so he could get into my car. The car had bucket seats and I had my briefcase on the passenger seat. I slowly put the briefcase down on the floor and moved over. The whole time my mind was racing, trying to think of what I could do."

The man climbed into Eddy's patrol car and shoved the butt of his gun into her ribs.

"He told me to give him my gun," she says. "I said, 'Okay,' but didn't move. He jammed his gun into my side a second time and said, 'I told you, *give me your gun!*'

"I still didn't move right away. I know it sounds silly but I thought, *I might die here, and if I get shot and killed, I don't want to die with my gun in its holster.* I knew that if I went for my gun really fast he'd kill me before I even got it out. So I started to pull it out slowly with my thumb and forefinger, figuring I'd have a better chance of using it if I got it out of my holster."

As Eddy began to pull out her gun, the suspect put the car into reverse and became confused.

"How do I get out of here?" he asked.

"Over there," she responded, pointing past his face and out the driver's side window. The suspect's gaze followed her hand. Eddy took advantage of this distraction. She quickly pushed his gun away from her ribs and jumped on top of him. As she did so, she tried to re-grip her own gun but it bounced out of her hand, landed on the man's lap, and dropped down into the door well.

"I grabbed his gun and tried to get it away from him," Eddy continues. "Suddenly the gun went off and he dropped it. I grabbed the radio and said, 'Robert 1 needs help.' Then the man reached down and found my gun in the door well. He came up with it and said, 'Okay, okay,' in a tone that suggested that now I was really going to get it. I put both of my hands on the gun and tried to gain control of it while he tried to point it at my face. Then my gun fired, sending a bullet into the door frame just above the guy's head."

As the two continued to struggle over her weapon, Eddy suddenly realized an even greater danger—the patrol car was rolling toward the river.

"I thought, *Oh, man, we're going to go into the water and we're going to die*," she recalls. "He must have thought the same thing because he suddenly jammed on the brakes just short of the river's edge."

Back in the struggle, Eddy fought hard to stop the man from pointing the gun directly at her face. Gradually, she turned the barrel toward the man by bending back his hand. With his hand bent, the man's trigger finger got pinched by the gun. He let out a cry of pain and released his hold on the weapon. Eddy reacted immediately.

"I grabbed the gun and shoved the barrel right behind his ear. I said, 'You're a fucker and I'm going to kill you!' And I was really about to kill him. Finally, he froze."

By this time, other officers had responded to the scene and heard the two gunshots, but they couldn't tell where the sounds came from. Eventually, one officer realized a struggle was going on inside the car. When he opened the door, he found Eddy holding the suspect at gunpoint. The officer dragged the man out of the car, threw him down onto the ground and handcuffed him.

Eddy emerged from her car, holstered her gun, and worked to regain her composure. She soon learned that the suspect had previously fired on the original chasing officer, and that a watch commander and shooting team had responded to investigate that earlier incident. They were unaware that Eddy had fought her own battle inside her patrol car until the watch commander came over to ask her how she apprehended the suspect.

"I started to explain what happened," she recalls, "and he looked at me with this kind of amazement on his face. The commander said, 'I had no idea that shots had been fired over here.' I said, 'Oh, I thought that was why you were talking to me.' 'No,' he replied, 'but go on.'

"That particular incident did more for my reputation than anything I could have ever accomplished. I got a lot of good feedback from my fellow officers, like one traffic officer came to me the next day and said, 'Hey, I heard about what happened to you last night. I'm really proud of you, you little shit.' And my lieutenant had me stand up at roll call the next night and tell everyone what happened."

The most surprising reaction, however, came from that sergeant who had once threatened to have her fired.

"He came up to me at the precinct," Eddy explains with a smile. "He wouldn't look at me, but he said, 'You know, you did one hell of a job out there.' Then he walked away."

Eddy is now a sergeant herself, and that fateful day in her patrol car proved to be a rite of passage. But it was not the first such moment for a female officer, and it would not be the last. Indeed, while women have served on police departments in the

United States since 1910, they have frequently faced discrimination and doubt about their abilities.

The earliest generations of female law enforcement officers were called "policewomen." In the years between World War I and the Vietnam War, they functioned more like detective-style social workers than beat cops, and they primarily worked to prevent child abuse, assist juveniles, and track runaways. Policewomen were segregated into women's divisions, were often paid less than their male counterparts, and were not allowed to test for the same promotions as the men.

The old ways began to change in the 1960s when lawsuits in several cities challenged the limited promotional opportunities for women. By the end of the decade, the segregation had ended, and policewomen began sitting for promotional exams alongside male officers. Suddenly, men in blue everywhere began to feel threatened by their female competitors. But that would not be the worst of it. One last bastion of maleness remained—the world of patrol—and when the door to that "boys only" club was opened in the mid-70s, a real battle of the sexes began. Not just because for the first time women were riding in squad cars with male partners and competing equally with them, but because in doing so they redefined what it meant to be a police officer. Now identified as "female officers," these women relied more on verbal skills and persuasion than on sheer brute force, and many men could not accept this approach.

The idea for *A Different Shade of Blue* first came to me when I was serving as a Seattle city prosecutor. One day in court, I struck up a conversation with a female police officer who had been patrolling the streets of Seattle for almost twenty years. She told me that when she began there were only a handful of women on the department.

I asked her, "Did you face a lot of prejudice from the male officers?"

"Oh, yeah," she replied. "The men were in three basic camps. Three quarters of the guys were fine and gave us a chance. Then there were the old-timers who wouldn't talk to us at all, and if they saw us in the hallway they made us walk around them. Then there was the third group who thought, 'Hey, they're here so we might as well *date* them!' "

Following that conversation, I researched the history of female cops and discovered Seattle was one of the first cities to hire policewomen in 1912. With its long history of being a trailblazer on women's issues, Seattle provides the perfect backdrop to tell this American story. Seattle's female citizens had the right to vote ten years before the 19th Amendment to the U.S. Constitution granted that right nationwide. In addition, in 1926 Seattle became the first major American city to elect a female mayor, and twenty years later the Seattle Police Department's Captain Irene Durham was the highest-ranking female police officer in the country.

Although women from the earliest era are no longer living, I interviewed female officers who hired on as far back as 1946 and up through the present day to get a complete picture of the challenges they have endured—from segregation and sexual harassment to the ongoing battle to break through the "glass ceiling."

Lis Eddy and the other Seattle women who share their stories in the following pages are all a part of the amazing national history of female police officers. They tell tales of humor and sadness, of fear and self-doubt mixed with great heroism. They also speak of the friendships they have made over the years, not just with other women, but with many men as well. As they recount their experiences, they prove that regardless of race, background, or sexual orientation, women are indeed a different shade of blue. And this difference has forever changed the face of police work.

1

IN THE DAYS OF SOILED DOVES AND LILY WAVERS

For policewoman Norma Wilson, the day's assignment sounded straightforward enough—check up on a man who had recently returned to his family after spending time in the state mental hospital. The man's wife was pregnant, and his trade union had convinced the doctors to release him so he could take care of her and their two kids.

Like other policewomen in the 1940s, Wilson left the downtown precinct dressed in plain clothes. She also was unarmed and drove in an unmarked patrol car. Normally, traveling incognito was not a problem; on this day, it proved to be a blessing. When she reached the family's address, she found a typical Seattle house built up off the street. She parked her car, and then climbed a long flight of stairs up to the front porch.

"When I got there, the husband greeted me at the door," Wilson explains. "He had blood all over him, and he held a butcher knife in his hand that was also covered in blood. He stared at me with this strange, distant expression on his face.

"I asked, 'Is everything all right?' He replied, 'Yes,' and continued to look at me with that distant stare. I said, 'Okay, well, you stay here and take care of everything.' He nodded his head, and I took off."

Wilson slowly backed down the stairs and went to call for help. This was in the days before two-way radios, and the unit in her car could only receive calls one-way from dispatch. To reach the station she had to use a call box several blocks away. She quickly walked to it, called in for backup, and returned to her car to wait.

"Within minutes, about eight squad cars came," she says. "I went in with the other officers—all male—and they immediately put handcuffs on the guy. Then we went into the bathroom and found the man's wife lying in the shower stall, bleeding from her neck. He had slit her throat. She was dead."

The family's two children were also inside the house; fortunately, they were unharmed. Wilson quickly hurried them out of the home and took them down to juvenile hall while the men waited for the coroner to arrive. Later, the mentally disturbed husband hanged himself in jail, and the children were placed into the custody of the wife's family.

"When I was at the door and first saw the husband with the knife," Wilson reflects, "I didn't identify myself as a police officer because I took one look at him and just knew something was terribly wrong. I didn't know what to say, but I knew I needed assistance. That's one of the things about police work. You had to make up your mind in a split second about what you were going to do. You really had to act fast. It wasn't a matter of being scared. I didn't have time. With the husband there wasn't anything else I could do but call for backup. This was back when we women didn't carry guns, and I certainly wasn't going to take that knife away from him."

Facing down a homicidal husband was the farthest thing from Wilson's mind when she walked into the Seattle Police Department for the first time in January, 1945. World War II was winding down to an Allied victory, and the attractive twenty-four-year-old brunette was searching for a way out of her boring, dead-end secretarial job at the Boeing Aircraft Company. There was a wartime hiring freeze on, however, and the only way to change jobs was to have a certificate of availability from your employer. Wilson didn't have one.

She considered relocating to Florida where her uncle operated a grain elevator, but then she learned about a civilian opening in the Seattle Police Department record's division. Police work was considered military for transfer purposes, and Wilson could obtain that certificate of availability if the police department hired her. She immediately went down to personnel, took a simple written exam, and was offered the job the very next day.

Stepping into the world of cops and criminals in the 1940s was like walking into a Hollywood gangster movie filled with rich characters and twisting plots. The setting for Wilson's new adventure was a six-story stone and brick triangular structure known as the Public Safety Building. In a bygone era, the first floor had housed stables for police horses. By the time Wilson arrived it had been remodeled to accommodate holding cells for criminals brought in by the Seattle Police Department's black paddy wagon nicknamed "The Black Mariah." The next several floors held the downtown precinct and the chief's office, while the two top floors housed the city hospital and jail. Once inside the precinct, Wilson found herself immersed in a world of strange police lingo and traditions.

"One day early on I was in the mug room looking at books of mugs shots," she notes. "The room had these tall, slanted desks on either side that you had to stand up at in order to look at the books. Under the pictures of some women were the words 'soiled dove,' and some of the men's pictures had the word 'lily waver' underneath them. I turned to the male detectives who were working at desks nearby and asked, 'What's a lily waver? What's a soiled dove?' The men looked at me and at each other, and then they just walked out of the room. The detectives were too embarrassed to explain that a soiled dove referred to a prostitute and that a lily waver was a man who exposed himself."

Wilson was hired to serve as a civilian in the records department, but her secretarial skills proved particularly valuable, and she soon was assigned to take statements for the vice squad and the chief of police. Gradually, she became interested in doing real police work. In 1946 the department announced it would hire several policewomen. Wilson applied and became one of five women to pass the required civil service test.

By a simple fluke of timing — she was working on the day the results were announced — Wilson became the first policewoman appointed after the Second World War. She was unique in another way. Although male officers needed only a high school diploma to get hired, policewomen were required to have a college degree. Wilson's secretarial skills proved so useful that the department waived the requirement, and she became the only woman granted that exception.

Becoming a policewoman in the forties was celebrated with little fanfare. There was no appointment ceremony, no congratulatory buffet or slaps on the back. Instead, "They just told us that we had passed the exam, handed us a badge, and sent us to work."

As Wilson soon learned, going to work meant more than just joining the Women's Bureau; it also meant becoming a part of an historic legacy that stretched back to the early days of the women's suffrage movement.

One of the most liberal cities in the nation, Seattle had a long history of supporting women's rights. In the 1910s, suffrage leaders such as Susan B. Anthony and O.H.P. Belmont frequently visited the Emerald City, paving the way for Washington state women to have the right to vote ten years before their counterparts nationwide. Over the next several decades, Seattle continued to be pivotal to the women's movement. In 1920, the League of Women Voters chose the city for its first national convention and, in 1926, Seattle elected the first female mayor of a major American city. Given this legacy, it was only natural that when those same suffrage leaders advocated the hiring of policewomen across the nation, Seattle quickly obliged.

The idea of women working in law enforcement was not a new one. As far back as the 1850s, they had been serving as jail and prison matrons for female arrestees and prisoners. By the early twentieth century women's rights advocates urged cities to hire policewomen because they saw male officers as unsympathetic to the plight of children and young women. Los Angeles is frequently credited with hiring the first full-time policewomen in 1910, but Seattle soon followed with five in 1912.

In the 1910s and '20s, Seattle's policewomen were assigned to the Women's Protective Division of the police department. Their job paid a salary of eighty-five dollars a month, and meant the "wearing of the 'star' and the authority to make arrests, just the same as any blue coat on the force." Once hired, the women made rescue work of children and young women the main focus of their police activities. They frequently traveled in pairs, patrolled dances attended by young people, and earned the nickname "The Purity Squad."

When Wilson became a policewoman, stories of the earliest policewomen continued to whisper through the rafters of the musty old precinct. The most celebrated was Sylvia Hunsicker, who was hired on in 1915. Known throughout the city as Mrs. Hunsicker, the stalwart policewoman became famous for walking a beat down in the shipyards where she looked out for "little tots who get lost on the docks while their parents are waiting for the arrival or departure of ships." She also kept a steady lookout for "young girls who come to the big city alone and don't know where to go." Seven years into her tenure she created her own makeshift uniform made up of a long coat and hat, both carrying the Seattle Police Department badge.

Wilson paid close attention to the tales of Mrs. Hunsicker because in years past her own parents had benefited from the early policewoman's good graces.

"During the depression years in the thirties, the Seattle city government ran out of money and city employees like police and fire received vouchers instead of paychecks," Wilson explains. "They had to go out and find people to cash the vouchers because there was no money in the city treasury to redeem them. My father was on the fire department so I know this happened. He and my mother used to go down to stores they knew would take the vouchers, and they would have to buy something in order to get the vouchers cashed. Mrs. Hunsicker had money. I don't know whether it was from what she had saved or because she got it from her family, but come pay day the guys would go down to the Women's Office and Mrs. Hunsicker would cash their checks."

Although Mrs. Hunsicker had long since retired by the time Wilson was appointed, there were several policewomen still active from that earlier era. The Woman's Protective Division had been reorganized into the Women's Bureau, and the youthful Wilson found herself working with an interesting mix of mostly older, married or widowed policewomen. Her first assignment was working with Fern Wheeler, who had joined the SPD in 1929. Wheeler had gained a reputation department-wide for her work on the Morals Detail—otherwise known as sex cases.

"The men called her 'Stern Wheeler.' " Wilson recalls. "She was a big woman with a loud voice. She was hard of hearing, and when she took statements over the telephone her voice was so loud the guys used to kid her and say, 'God, why don't you just open a window and yell out. You don't need to use the phone, because we can all hear you.' While on the phone, Fern would shout, 'He did *what* to you? *How?*'

"Fern was also an astrologer and believed in reincarnation. She actually wrote books about astrology and she forecast the future based on the stars and when you were born. I don't know how old Fern was when she finally retired, but before she left, she'd gotten to know me pretty well and she told me about going to church one day and talking to a famous person. She said she was talking over her shoulder to him and somebody behind her said, 'Are you talking to me?' And Fern said, 'Of course not. I'm talking to King George.' I told her, 'I don't think you'd better tell those stories around here, Fern.' "

While Wheeler herself proved to be comical, the Morals Detail cases were often very serious, and Wilson soon found herself helping the policewoman/astrologer investigate rape charges and allegations of incest and sexual abuse.

"It was really different in those days," Wilson reflects. "Sometimes we had to pick up the kids if their fathers or stepfathers were molesting them. We had to get them away from their family and let the court decide where they belonged. Initially the mothers would agree that their husband should be charged with a crime and that their child should be removed and protected. Then, later, when the women were back at home, they'd start thinking about how they were going to pay the bills if their husband was in jail. I used to get so mad because nine times out of ten the mothers would change their minds about prosecution. Many times the mothers would be back at the precinct the next day, wanting to talk their child into changing her story.

"The children were often sacrificed. The most difficult part was when the sex crimes cases went to state court. In those days there weren't any rules protecting kids who had to testify against their parents or against someone who had molested them. Defense attorneys defended their clients any way they could, and if that meant scaring the poor kids to death, well, that was all right. I hated the way the kids were treated. And the courts were not taking the charges very seriously. The guys would often get thirty days suspended, which meant no time in jail. I asked one of the judges about that, and he said 'There is no room for them. We have to decide who to let out, and you just kind of hope this doesn't occur again.'

"I advised one parent not to press charges," Wilson adds. "The defendant didn't rape her daughter but he did molest her to some degree. The little girl was so scared. I had been there quite a while at that point and I just couldn't see this poor kid standing up there testifying. Finally, I said to her mother, 'It's not going to be worth it. Your kid would be more traumatized than any sentence the guy was going to get.' "

Although Wilson would continue to work on abuse cases throughout her career, she quickly grew weary of being exclusively assigned to the Morals Detail.

"After six months of talking about nothing but sex, and how big it was and what he did with it and all the rest of it, I said, 'You're either going to transfer me out of here and let somebody else take a turn at it or I'm going to quit.' So they allowed me to work on other cases and they started passing the morals work around."

As Wilson gained wider exposure to Women's Bureau cases, she encountered various forms of relationship abuse, now commonly referred to as domestic violence. Today, most cities have mandatory arrest policies in domestic violence cases, and prosecutors proceed to trial with or without the victim's cooperation. In Wilson's day, however, victims controlled the prosecution. Cases would be dismissed if the victim decided to drop the charges, and policewomen were frequently frustrated by women who changed their minds about holding their husbands or lovers accountable.

"Most of the time I would get mad at the women because they wouldn't prosecute no matter what the guys did," Wilson explains. "I'd get so damned disgusted that I'd say, 'You know there's going to come a time when you're just going to get killed. Are you sure you don't want to press charges?' If the woman said 'No,' there was usually nothing we could do. And, of course, even if the women did initially file a complaint, they would be right down the next hour bailing the guy out.

"I had one case where I got to know the woman real well," she adds. "Her name was Alice and her husband was a drunk.

He beat her, and he would pick up their welfare check and spend it on drink. She was often out begging for food. I really felt sorry for that gal because she was limited herself, and she had three or four boys and a girl. They were good kids and she really loved them, but she was always struggling to make ends meet. Although she was never arrested, she was always under investigation for neglect. I remember she would go downtown to get some kerosene to warm up her house, and she would call me and I'd send a district car to give her a ride home. Alice was just one of those people I'd watch out for and try to help when I could.

"One day she got pregnant again and landed in the hospital. I got a call to go interview her because they thought she'd tried to kill herself. She wouldn't tell her doctors what happened, but when I asked she said, 'God, with what I've been through I didn't want to bring another kid into the world. So I took a coat hanger and did it myself. But nothing happened.' On the day of my interview, the baby aborted. Alice then explained, 'You know, I was so curious I turned it over to see what sex it was, and it was another boy.' Abortion was illegal in those days, and she turned to me and said, 'You won't tell on me, will you?' I said, 'No.' And I never did."

Following close on Wilson's heels was newspaper reporter Jean Selvidge Dunbar, whose route to becoming a working policewoman was also circuitous. Like Wilson, World War II had offered Dunbar a unique opportunity—to become a beat reporter for *The Seattle Star* newspaper right out of journalism school. She got her big break because many of the regular male reporters were either serving in the military or covering the war. One of her primary assignments was the police beat, and she quickly got to know many of the officers on a first-name basis.

"Those were the days of wild reporting and some great newspaper men," Dunbar recalls over a cup of coffee at her home in the seaside town of Port Orchard, Washington. "The pressroom in the old triangle building was an entity unto itself. The precinct was filled with mice, and the reporters had names for all of them. They even had a party for a mouse named Henrietta when she got pregnant. And the relationship between police and reporters was totally different back then. Right after they put radios in police cars, two reporters named Johnnie Redding and Bob Lloyd stole a police car. They were drunk, of course, and they went driving madly all over the city, coming onto the radio and taunting the radio operator. Nothing was ever done about it. The police were our buddies, and usually stood right behind us, and we covered for them a lot too. That was another day and time."

When the war ended, Dunbar initially stayed on at *The Star* while others got their pink slips, but her fortunes soon changed when the paper was sold and subsequently closed. As she was contemplating her future, the Seattle Police Department approached her to head up a new unit called the Public Information Office (PIO) to serve as the department's first public-relations person.

"I didn't give it much thought at first," she recalls, "but then I thought, well, everybody hates cops, or at least there was a real apathy towards them. As a journalist covering the courts and the police beat, I knew an awful lot of police officers and I had the utmost respect for a lot of them, especially the detectives who I considered to be the cream of the crop. No one had ever tried to improve their public image, and I thought this would be a real challenge."

Dunbar accepted the position and prepared to leap in with both feet. The department was not allowed to hire a civilian expert in those days, so she was officially hired under the umbrella of the Women's Bureau. She became the only policewoman ever appointed to work in a non-policewoman capacity.

"I loved working in the Public Information Office," Dunbar says. "The best part was public contact and working with the media. Not with the day-to-day coverage of the police department, but on special programs like the Dangerous Stranger Program where I would go out to day camps and to schools to tell children to beware of strangers. At that time the department had an orchestra, and we set up a school assembly program that was both entertaining and educational. We also set up a pedestrian safety school for adult jaywalkers that we ran two or three times a month in the evening. I also started an internal newsletter called *The Call Box*, and ghost-wrote articles for the chief."

Although she found the public relations work challenging, after four years with the PIO Dunbar yearned to do real police work and transferred over to the Women's Bureau to become a regular policewoman. Dunbar's timing proved fortunate because soon after her transfer, the department started sending policewomen through the police academy.

The decision to send women to the academy followed on the heels of the decision to arm them with guns. Initially, the policewomen were given firearms with little training. Then, as rumor has it, one day one of the older policewomen, B.J. Bjornson, was seen waving her gun in the air across the street from the precinct. The department brass quickly decided to send all policewomen through formal training.

"We went through firearms certification with the rest of the academy class, and were qualified to carry small .38 caliber pistols," Dunbar says. "But they wouldn't let us qualify with the shotgun because they didn't want the liability. Apparently one of the early policewomen raised hell because she thought she would suffer injury to her breasts from the shotgun. That was, of course, completely ridiculous. You won't suffer an injury from firing a shotgun if you're properly taught and use it correctly."

Once out on the streets, Dunbar quickly realized that the men on the department relied heavily on the work of the Women's Bureau.

"I never had problems with the male officers and detectives," she notes. "They were glad to have us because they could use us in a lot of situations. For instance, we did all of the child neglect cases, which we referred to as 'injurious living' crimes. Those cases were very difficult for the men to take. Many of them couldn't handle seeing children sleeping in a bed with lice and insects and grubs and feces. Child assaults were also very difficult for many male officers. They couldn't handle seeing the bruises, like the belt marks on the backs of kids. I've watched men cry when they've seen a child badly abused and beaten. I remember one time we were waiting for the father or the boyfriend to come home so we could arrest him for assaulting a child. I had to ask the sergeant to get the other male officer out of the house because he was so livid I was afraid that if the suspect walked in he'd clobber him. I think the men were very glad when we showed up and took over the handling of those kinds of investigations.

"I never felt resentment from the fellows," she adds. "The only thing they resented was I always opened my own doors. I'll never forget during a narcotics raid at the old US Hotel. Carl Meyer was a good narcotics officer, and we went in on this raid together. I started charging through the front door and, all of a sudden, this great big hand grabbed me by the waist and just picked me up and set me back outside the door. They were very protective of the policewomen."

Among Dunbar's favorite assignments was working undercover on sting operations.

"Most of the policewomen were married and had kids, and they resented the special assignments," she explains. "But I was single for years and I loved special details like working narcotics and being an undercover plant. I thought it was the greatest part of police work and, despite the seriousness of our jobs, we tried to have fun when we could.

"I remember one time we had a rapist up on the hill who was attacking people while they sat in their parked cars. His modus operandi was to take a four-door car, go to the back right rear door which was oftentimes unlocked, and climb in with his .45 caliber pistol. He would put the .45 on the couple in the front seat and order them to have intercourse, and then he would rape the woman. Sometimes he'd pistol whip the guy. He didn't kill anybody, but he did commit quite a few rapes. The department had about three or four teams of us out trying to catch the guy. At roll call, the teams were lined up and Captain Charlie Rouse briefed us on the assignment. The Captain asked if there were any questions. I asked, 'Is the uniform of the day chastity belt snuggies?' In my mind, you had to have a sense of humor."

Besides narcotic and other special details, the policewomen also worked on prostitution stings.

"In those days we knew all the prostitutes and madams by name," Dunbar says. "There was one prostitute named Titsy Russell. She was a wonderfully tall, stately gal with a degree of class. I'll never forget, one night I was driving down the street and a car pulled up next to mine. The john was a short little guy. He was driving, and Titsy was sitting in the passenger seat, all dressed up and towering over him. I looked at her and she looked at me. I smiled and she just started to laugh. We both knew what was going on.

"We also had some great madams. One was a cook who had a successful Italian restaurant that she ran for a long time. Like the other madams, she used the jail for recruiting. When we picked up one of her girls, she'd come and retrieve them and say to us, 'You have your job, and I have mine.' "

"Of course, many of these women led very sad lives," she adds. "One gal I remember in particular went by the name Sheila. She was a beautiful black woman from a good Seattle family who got into drugs and prostitution. Over the years Sheila was in and out of Western State Mental Hospital and in and out of jail. She was so gorgeous that psychiatrists fell madly in love with her. She was the first black woman I saw in a blonde wig, and she had a beautiful body and a beautiful carriage. I told her, 'You are so gorgeous, and with your personality, you could do so many things.' From time to time she managed to pull herself out of that lifestyle, but she always ended up getting back into drugs.

"Years later, not too long before I retired, I went on a raid with the narcotics unit. We were moving really fast inside this apartment, trying to gather the evidence before they flushed the drugs down the toilet. I looked over and saw this lump of a human being sitting on a sofa in the corner of the room. It was dark and I wasn't paying attention. I turned to one of the detectives and I said, 'Tanner, who's that in the corner?' And he said 'Jean, take another look.' It was Sheila. Her good looks were gone, and she was just completely destroyed."

Although many of their cases revealed the harsher sides of life, policewomen had their share of humorous and oddball investigations. One of Dunbar's more unusual cases involved gypsies who worked in the once-illegal racket called fortunetelling.

"We had one family called the Stevensons who were always into scams of all sorts," she says. "I remember one time detective Dewey Gillespie and I went out to have our fortunes told. Our cover story was that we were having marital problems and we went and asked what we should do. We paid twenty-five dollars for the big candle and everything. The fortuneteller spoke to us together and she talked to us separately. One of the things she suggested was that I should enhance my breasts because I was very skinny. I had been on the department for fifteen to eighteen years by then, and the following day I went to work and put balloons in my bra. The chief of police happened to walk into the Women's Bureau and was just incensed when he saw me. He didn't think it was proper at all, but everybody else thought it was hilarious.

"Fortunetelling was considered a form of fraud back then," Dunbar adds. "But she was right about my breasts. I was pretty flat-chested."

Breasts came up again in the line of duty when there was a sudden increase in the theft of a particular style of women's garment.

"Cashmere sweaters became very popular among young women in the fifties," Dunbar recalls. "We worked closely with the counselors in the schools and this one middleschool counselor called me and needed help because several young girls were getting involved in shoplifting. So policewoman Pat Mikkelborg and I went out and spent a whole day with the little girls and the counselors. By the end of the day, Pat and I were just giggling idiots because these little middleschool girls would all come in with their falsies on. There was one little girl who you would swear wore pinecones for falsies because one boob pointed straight up while the other boob stuck straight out. It just made us laugh. Police work can have some bad moments, but there were a lot of amusing moments too."

Both Wilson and Dunbar retired from the Seattle Police Department at the end of the 1960s, though they left for different reasons. During the middle years of her career, Wilson married a police sergeant who subsequently died tragically of a heart attack. In 1969, she married a businessman from Hawaii and retired to live with him in Honolulu. There, she became a renaissance woman of sorts, delving into painting while also dabbling in real estate.

Dunbar also married a police officer while on the department. She continued to work until 1968 when she accidentally fell down a flight of stairs in her backyard and broke her back. She eventually recovered and later returned to police-type work in the early 1970s for a brief time as a probation officer in Juvenile Hall.

"I never intended to work for a long time at the police department," Wilson notes in retrospect. "The job started out as just a means to get out of my position at Boeing, and as a way to have a job until something else came along. But that never happened, and I stayed with the SPD. In the end, I really liked working with the people."

"I've heard people say, 'Well in those days you didn't do *real* police work," Dunbar adds. "The hell we didn't. I worked homicides, burglaries, robberies, rapes, and served as undercover plants. On Friday and Saturday nights, we also patrolled juvenile hangouts. The years I served as a policewoman were the greatest years of my life. You never knew from one day to the next what would happen during your day. I loved the challenge, and it was a great job."

2

SOCIAL WORK WITH A GUN AND A BADGE

For most policewomen, the day-to-day life of being a cop rarely offered the opportunity to solve famous crimes or to create newspaper headlines. And, although they regularly traveled in some of the city's most dangerous neighborhoods and faced real dangers on a daily basis, few had the chance over the course of their careers to save the day on a grand scale.

Take, for example, Mary Robinson. She first hired on with the SPD in 1955, left the department in 1962 to raise her children, returned in 1970, and retired sixteen years later after earning the rank of sergeant.

"As a policewoman, I didn't do any heroics so I don't have any stories like that," Robinson says. "But I do remember incidents, vignettes. Vignettes are what life is made up of and, often, those are the memories that come back to you years later.

"One particular incident that impressed me occurred while I was doing court duty in the 1950s: I talked to a woman who had killed her live-in boyfriend. I'm not very good with ages, but I would say she was middle-aged, and I remember she was African American. She was in jail while the prosecutors were trying to decide what crime they were going to charge her with."

Robinson was sent up to interview the female suspect in the jail. To her surprise, the woman confessed her guilt and was forthcoming with the details of her crime.

"The woman told me that her boyfriend had repeatedly abused her," the veteran policewoman recalls. "On the day of the murder, she'd had enough and stabbed him to death with a butcher knife. But fifteen minutes had transpired between the time she picked up the knife and the time she started stabbing him. This was before the battered women's syndrome had become a recognized legal defense, and the prosecutors were grappling with whether there was the premeditation for first degree murder, or whether she should be charged with second degree murder or manslaughter.

"Despite her confession, I didn't get the sense that she belonged in jail. I mean, she did kill the guy. That was not the question. But the woman did not have a criminal record, and I will never forget the look on her face. She was in a daze, in a complete state of shock. You could see it on her face, in her body language, everything. And she kept saying, 'This is so unreal. I just don't believe this. I feel like this is a bad dream and I'll wake up in a few minutes. Then I don't, and I'm still here, and I've still done this terrible thing.' "

Robinson never saw the woman again after that day. She later learned the defendant was charged with manslaughter, but never discovered her ultimate fate. Still, the look on the murderess's face continues to haunt the policewoman to this day.

"After I got through talking to her, I remember walking out of there thinking what a fine line there was between her side of the table and mine. I mean, in just one split second things can happen that will change your entire life.

"Years later, in my own marriage I had occasion to find myself that angry," Robinson adds. "Fortunately, I didn't happen to pick up a knife and stab my husband, but I was shocked because I had never experienced that kind of anger in all my years of growing up. It was really scary and it made me think of her again. There is such a fine line."

As the 1950s unfolded, the policewomen of the Women's Bureau found themselves facing many fine lines—the line that isolated them from the male officers and detectives, the one that distinguished them from social workers of the day, and the one that separated them from the public.

With post-war prosperity, younger and predominantly single women were hired to replace the older generation of policewomen and to fill out the growing ranks of the Women's Bureau. Among the first was Helen Karas. Hired in 1951, Karas was a "tough broad" in the best sense of the word, a dogged crime fighter who would stop at nothing to bag her man.

"Helen was sharp, and when she first came on she was *very* enthusiastic," laughs Norma Wilson, who was a five-year veteran on the department when Karas arrived. "Helen knew what to look for and she was good. She would see people blocks away doing an illegal turn, and she would honk her horn and yell, 'What are you doing, you SOB?' I would say, 'Karas, he can't hear you and you can't do anything about it. So, shut up!' She would get so mad at people that she would threaten to arrest them, and I'd say, 'What are you going to arrest them for?' She wouldn't have an answer. I'd say, 'You don't threaten people with anything unless you know what you can do. You've got to face the judge. What are you going to tell him? What law are they breaking?' I told her, 'You can't go around doing that. Just hold back and do a little more investigation.' Boy, she was tough."

Karas quickly became legendary in the department. Many male officers and policewomen alike would tell the tale of her encounter with two drunken sailors in a bar who were embroiled in a fistfight. When the sailors wouldn't calm down, she took each of them by the scruff of their necks and banged their heads together.

Then there was the time Karas was riding in a squad car and suddenly spotted a delinquent teenager on the street.

"She was a runaway we'd handled innumerable times from the state school for girls," recalls Karas. "I was wearing a skirt and I had on heels. I just stopped the car, took off my shoes and ran after her. I chased her about eight blocks. I was in good shape in those days and I could move pretty fast.

"Before becoming a policewoman I worked in juvenile detention down in Santa Barbara, California," she adds, "and a superintendent told me if a kid tries to run you stand still, call them every name in the book and they'll stop. So when I got close enough to her, I started calling her names. I told her she was a miserable son of a bitch and she had better stop or I was going to clobber her. And she did stop. That was one thing that especially worked on boys. If a woman starts swearing at them, they can't believe it. They aren't expecting it, and it stops them long enough that you can usually grab them."

Karas also worked undercover as a prostitute for three weeks to take down an illegal bookmaking operation involving the horse races.

"My cover name was 'Leslie Erickson,' and I claimed to be a call girl from San Francisco," she says. "Everybody on the department was told that if they saw me anywhere they were to pretend like they didn't know me. I became a call girl because that way I would fit in with the bookie crowd, and that was the only thing that we could think of. I had a sergeant and a captain who were paying very close attention to me and I had to report to them almost every twenty-four hours. I would give them my notes, identifying the people and other information about the operation.

"Acting like a prostitute was very simple. I had been associating with prostitutes for quite a while as a policewoman, and I knew I should just act normal. According to my cover I had a boyfriend who was coming up from San Francisco and I couldn't work until he arrived. The bookies respected that, but one of the night clerks who lived in the hotel invited me up to his room late one evening. I'd already turned him down about fifty times and I knew I couldn't keep refusing, so I went up to his room. He was drinking straight whiskey. He kept filling my glass, but I poured it down the sink as fast as I could every time his back was turned. Fortunately, he finally passed out. The fact that I went up to his room helped my cover. Nobody else pressed me to perform and, since I was also placing bets, the bookies accepted me."

As the undercover operation continued, Karas's "boyfriend" — played by an old-time cop named Pee Wee Hughes—"came up from San Francisco" to see why she wasn't regularly sending down her earnings.

"Unfortunately, Pee Wee looked too much like a cop and the bookies didn't like him. So we had to get rid of him. He and I staged a big fight in front of everyone. He wasn't too much taller than I was, and we stood there and went at each other tooth-and-nail. Then he stomped out. Of course, we made certain the hotel clerk and one of the fellows who carried the betting slips were there to witness our argument. At that point, we figured we could lose Pee Wee because the undercover was only going to last a few more days and I'd be okay.

"We had the bookies tighter than a drum," Karas notes. "But the prosecuting attorney turned out to be crooked as all get out. We had a perfect case on eight different people for bookmaking on horses, and we were going to send detectives out to make the arrest at the location where the bookies had their phones and records. But the prosecutor insisted on holding a press conference first, and when our guys got out to the place to make the arrests no one was there. Fortunately, they left behind all the betting slips, including the ones I had used, and I had photographs and notes on all the activities. So we still had a good case, and they all went to jail.

"The sad part was the prosecuting attorney in those days was right in with all of the bad guys," she adds. "That was the climate in Seattle at that time. I had another good case on a local gangster named Frank Colacurcio, and he was caught in bed with a fifteen-year-old runaway. His girlfriend was also in the bed, and she got mad at him and gave a statement. I also had a statement from the runaway, and both the runaway and the girlfriend had taken polygraphs. It was a solid case of carnal knowledge. But we took it over to the prosecutor and he said we didn't have enough evidence. The whole bunch of us got hauled into prosecutor Carroll's office to be told what was wrong with our case and why he couldn't prosecute it. After we walked out of his office, I kept my mouth shut about what happened because I didn't want to screw up my job. But from then on I knew the score, and every time he ran for prosecutor I didn't vote for him. He graduated from the University of Washington and was a football player, all those good things, and here he was protecting the slime of the earth."

As the Women's Bureau continued to expand, new policewomen came on the scene, including Karen Ejde, Mary Robinson, Beryl Thompson, and Noreen Skagen. In addition, Lillian Mitchell hired on in 1955 and became the first and only African American to serve as a policewoman on the department. Future true crime writer Ann Rule, author of *The Stranger Beside Me* and *Small Sacrifices*, among others, also served—on a provisional basis—for fourteen months, until she was released due to poor eyesight.

Of all the women hired during the 1950s, Karas became closest to Karen Ejde, and the two made the most unlikely of friends. While Karas was short, stout, and best described as a fiery Greek, Ejde was tall, lanky, and a more reserved, thoughtful Norwegian—back in the days when such ethnic differences were readily acknowledged. Their friendship endured for more than fifty years, and in retirement they lived in adjoining houses on five tree-covered acres on Washington State's Olympic Peninsula.

Like many of her fellow policewomen, Ejde was initially attracted to the job because it offered steady work, excellent benefits, and a salary that was considerably higher than she could earn as a schoolteacher or social worker. Even so, not everyone in Ejde's family appreciated her desire to fight crime.

"My mother didn't like my doing police work at all and never did," Ejde says. "She thought it was unseemly for a woman, especially a lady, to have such a career. Part of it may have been her upbringing in another culture—she was from Norway—and she may have thought it simply was not suitable for her daughter. Sure, she was a little old fashioned by today's standards, but that was the way she was. My father was reluctant at first to speak out about it until he and my mother had moved back to Norway. When he did speak, he went so far as to say, 'It's an honorable job, and you do good work. You certainly have, from a materialistic standpoint, good benefits and good pay. You'd better stay with it.' I think a lot of his attitude had to do with the fact that I hadn't married, and I needed that kind of stability and security. He was looking out for my future best interests, and he felt there was nothing to be ashamed of in being a policewoman."

As in earlier years, policewomen appointed in the 1950s were college graduates, most with degrees in social work. Since male police officers were routinely hired with only high school diplomas, the Women's Bureau was the most educated division in the Seattle Police Department. Before being hired, the women were also required to take a written civil service exam, a physical test, and satisfy certain height requirements.

"The physical test was very strenuous," recalls Noreen Skagen, who became a policewoman in 1959. "We had to run six flights of stairs in so many seconds while carrying a weight similar to that of a heavy fire department hose. We had to do sit-ups and pushups. I got all through the test and I was very surprised that I had passed. Then they put me on a scale and said, 'Well, now we'll take your height measurements.' When I was hired, you had to be 5'4" tall. Well, I was a hair over 5'3", and I thought, *This is it.* But the examiner at the time had an idea. We were in the old courthouse gym, and it had pipes running across the ceiling. She piled up a bunch of chairs so I could reach the pipes and told me to hang there as long as I could stand it. I hung on for a while, got on the scale, and I was 5'4" and a quarter. It really does work because as you hang your whole body stretches. That's how I got on the department!

"I felt a little in over my head at first," she adds. "Police work was one of the most difficult jobs to learn because of all the regulations and laws and paperwork forms. Fortunately, when you were first hired you were assigned to another policewoman who was experienced, and she taught you all you needed to know in terms of how to handle situations. And once you'd gone through the academy, you felt much more comfortable with what you were doing, and then they let you work a lot more on your own."

The women went through academy training six to twelve months after being hired. At the academy, they suddenly found themselves learning side-by-side with male patrol officers. This coed training represented one of the few times the policewomen were freed from the segregated world of the Women's Bureau.

"The academy back then was in the police building downstairs in a couple of classrooms," Ejde recalls. "The only time we weren't down there listening to lectures and taking tests was when we had our firearms training for a week out at the state academy. The men also had some physical training—swimming and playing basketball—but the women were not included in that."

"In my academy class the women wanted to do the physical training too so the men wouldn't be able to say we couldn't," adds Mary Robinson. "To some extent there was a slight tension between the women and the men. It was insidious, not something you could point to and say this or that happened. It was like any form of discrimination. I don't think it even was discrimination because we were well treated. But it was a kind of head-patting attitude, like 'They're here, we're stuck with them, so we may as well make it work.' "

"How men treated women in the academy varied from individual to individual," notes Beryl Thompson, who joined the SPD in 1958. "Some were very supportive, some were just kind of accepting, and a very few were standoffish. Of course, I could say the same thing was true after starting work on the job itself."

Once their academy training was completed, the women went back to the segregated world of the Women's Bureau, a status quo that was comfortable for both the men and the women.

"In those days, we were not a threat to the men," Thompson says, "because we were not able to compete with them for the same positions on the department or for the same promotions. I think the women, wherever they were assigned, did their jobs well, went along with the system, and didn't complain. That's just the way things were at that time. Maybe we should have pushed harder, but we didn't."

"You must look at how we grew up," Ejde explains. "We didn't push hard because we were of an age that grew up in the Depression, and our parents taught us to look for security. There were a lot of things that happened to us or that we were witness to that we chose not to make waves about because subconsciously we in our back of our minds we were thinking, *Can I afford to lose this job?* We were not of the newer generation that, according to statistics, changes their jobs at least seven times before they retire. That would not have occurred to us."

"I don't think there was a thought in anyone's mind at that time that women should be police officers with the same responsibilities as the men," Noreen Skagen adds. "When I was hired, the mentality at that time could not even comprehend a woman in a police uniform in a marked patrol car responding to calls like male police officers. I had no problems with that because I was of that generation. I probably would have questioned the job if it had been in-uniform patrol, because to society at the time it was totally unthinkable."

Although changing society's notions of a woman's place in police work may have been unthinkable at that time, the women were still very much aware of the inequities they faced. Besides earning lower pay than men with the same number of years on the force, they also had few opportunities to advance. While men were able to take promotional examinations and move up throughout the department, policewomen were restricted to promotion within the Women's Bureau, where there was only one captain and at most two sergeant positions. Years later, Karas, Ejde, Skagen and Thompson would become part of a revolution that would greatly expand the opportunities for women in police work, but in the 1950s they had to accept the status quo.

Many of the policewomen no doubt took their cues from the two women who supervised the Women's Bureau up into the mid-1950s — Captain Irene Durham and Sergeant Helen Elliott. Both had spent years learning how to navigate the male-dominated world of police work. Durham, in particular, had been very successful. She hired on in 1926 with a Bachelor's degree in journalism and a Master's in social work, and quickly rose up the ranks. In 1933 she was promoted to sergeant and supervisor of all the policewomen; in 1940, she was appointed captain. When she became chief of the Crime Prevention Unit in 1946 she was the highest ranking woman police officer in the United States, and possibly the only woman at that time to supervise both a women's unit and the all-male Vice Squad.

"I knew Irene really well because both of us were journalism graduates," Jean Selvidge Dunbar explains. "Irene was well respected inside the department. She was also politically well connected. She was a good friend of city councilmen and of the school board, and maintained public contact with a lot of different city and university groups."

By the 1950s, Captain Durham had turned the Women's Bureau into a top unit and her policewomen into cool professionals. Perhaps the most visible transformation occurred in 1953, when the women were issued police uniforms that served to further distinguish them from their male counterparts.

"At that time no one ever considered the idea that we should wear pants and a gun belt like the men," says Ejde. "Instead, they dressed us in dark blue skirts and jackets, a hat and high heels, and we carried our guns in a specially designed purse. While the outfit may have looked professional, it wasn't terribly practical for most policewoman duties. Imagine every summer being out at Stan Sears Hydroplane Racing Pits handling the lost and found children and trying to deal with ten to twelve kids who are sticky from ice cream and here you are in a skirt and heels. It was miserable."

While Captain Durham was in charge of the Women's Bureau, she left the day-to-day supervision of the unit to Sergeant Elliott, a woman the rank-and-file found to be very efficient and compassionate. Officially, she was called Sergeant Elliott, but to her policewomen she was known as "Mrs. Elliott."

"You have to realize that we're of the generation that recognizes that there are women and there are ladies," Ejde explains. "All ladies are women, but not all women are ladies. And Mrs. Elliott was a real lady. By her own actions, by the way she expressed herself. I never heard her raise her voice or scream or yell at anyone. I feel blessed that I got to work with Mrs. Elliott during my first year before she retired.

"I always hark back to one situation. I had been on the department probably three months when I was sent to a woman's house out in the projects that was a classic example of child neglect. I knew she was on welfare, and yet I saw men's shoes under the bed and encountered enough evidence to make it very plain that she was not using her welfare checks to take care of her kids. Instead, she was spending the money on booze and on her boyfriend. And she didn't seem to care. I went back to the office and went to see Mrs. Elliott. I said, 'Here she is, she's on welfare, and she is abusing the system.'

"Mrs. E. called me into her little glass-enclosed cubicle office, shut the door, and told me to sit down. She then proceeded to tell me the facts of life with regard to public assistance. She said, 'You are going to encounter many more like her, but there are many others who you'll never hear about who receive assistance, who accepted it for all the right reasons, and who are trying to better themselves. What you need to realize is that with any system like welfare, in order to help the maximum number of people who need the help and who deserve the help, you're going to have some who benefit but don't deserve to. They may technically need the assistance, but they don't use it in the right way.' She then said, 'Life's like that. You have to understand this. It's like what Lincoln said, 'We try to do the most good for the most people most of the time.' And that's what you're trying to do with welfare.' Her advice kept me in good stead in many situations after that."

The advice was particularly relevant for Ejde and the other policewomen because aiding welfare mothers and children in distress was a large part of their duties in the fifties. This was in the days before most cities had established formal child protection services, and the policewomen often found themselves handling allegations of child neglect, which the police department labeled "injurious living" cases.

"We did a better job than the welfare department did at that time," Karas says. "It was social work with a gun and a badge, and we had a very different kind of authority when we walked in the door. The welfare department had to call and make an appointment, but we could just show up, knock on the door, and go in. Back then, we would get a report that somebody was shacked up with somebody, and that their kids were neglected. So we'd go out and knock on the door. When they opened the door, we'd invite ourselves in and tell them why we were there. In those days we could check the icebox, the closet, under the bed, or anywhere else in the house without a search warrant. The houses we usually investigated were pigsties that stunk to high heaven.

On the first visit, we'd tell them to get their act together because we would be back, and if it was still a mess they'd be going to jail. And we did check back and make arrests when necessary."

"We really took on the burden of the welfare of all the children at risk in the city," Noreen Skagen adds. "A lot of people accused us of doing social work, which was fine, but we made a lot of arrests. In those days, most people weren't that aware of child abuse, and if they were, they would usually say it was the parents' responsibility. With the community very apathetic to what we were doing, these little kids were really out there with nobody looking after their welfare but twenty-one policewomen.

"I remember one case where a babysitter walked into the home where she was supposed to work one night and was so horrified by the conditions that she immediately called the police. We went out and found a home that was just unbelievably filthy, and three little kids that had been terribly neglected. The mother had gone out on a date. When she came home, she pulled into her driveway and I was standing there ready to meet her. The house was on one of our famous Seattle hills and when I opened her car door, a bunch of beer cans fell out and started rolling down the street. I told her to get out of the car, and I told her new boyfriend to go to a store down the street and get some soap. The male patrol officers we'd called as backups were in the backyard getting sick. It was horrible. Garbage and excrement everywhere."

"Going into homes where children have been neglected for long periods of time you find all kinds of human and animal feces and spoiled food," recalls Mary Robinson. "The first thing that hit you as you entered the doorway was the smell. At least, that was true for me, and I quickly learned to breathe through my mouth. We used to say we wished we could bottle the smells to take them into court, because as unpleasant as the sights might be in a photograph, they were nothing compared to the odor.

"The most depressing case I remember was one where a newborn baby died from neglect. The child was malnourished, had ulcerated sores all through the diaper area, and obviously had not been cared for. The parents just seemed to be totally unaware of their responsibility. We said, 'Didn't you see a diaper rash before it got to this point?' They said, 'Well, yeah, and I tried to do something about it but it just didn't seem to work.' They didn't get it at all."

"It was unbelievable what some of these houses looked like," Skagen says. "We all crawled into attics and got out kids who were in terrible shape. They were grim, very grim. We'd hear about them because somebody like a neighbor would call and say they'd heard a child crying or calling out. Somebody would finally decide that they couldn't let this go on any longer. We would go out there and see squalor and filth like nothing you could ever imagine. We had kids tied to cribs, and houses where the children had no food to eat. It was heartbreaking, and some of the children did not survive or we found them dead. If they were alive, we could take the child out of the environment, get them into a nice clean place—the youth center at that time had a place with nurses on duty for dependent and delinquent children—and the child would be cleaned up and cared for. Quite often that would lead to a placement in a foster home. Sometimes they would be totally taken away from their parents and put into adoption.

"Not all stories had unhappy endings," she adds. "We received a call that two little twin boys, newborn babies, were being abused by their mother. When I investigated, I found a house that was absolutely filthy. And there were these two beautiful little twin boys on beds with no sheets on the mattresses, and the kids had obviously just been left on the beds without adequate care. The mother was just in tears, and she told me that the day after the babies were born, her husband had walked out. She was eighteen years old, and she didn't have the foggiest idea of how to take care of babies. The house was filthy, and all she would do was cry. I spent quite a bit of time there with her. I called the visiting nurse and had her come out, and I went down to the store, got some soap, and we cleaned the house up. I also got a hold of the girl's father who lived in the city and told him what was happening. About a month later, I went back and the young mother was enjoying her babies, the nurse was coming out two or three times a week to help her care for them, and that case was closed. She was a caring, loving mother who just couldn't cope."

Besides the child neglect cases, the policewomen spent a considerable part of their days tracking down runaways.

"In those days there weren't that many kids out on the streets," says Karas, "and if they were out we knew why and where. At that time, kids could be arrested for delinquency if they were on the street during the school day or at night after the curfew. So we were out at night looking for kids, and checking out their hangouts. We seldom had runaways or escapees from the state juvenile school that were missing in our area longer than a month. We knew where to watch for them, and most of them were very familiar to us. These days there are no such juvenile laws, and kids can be anywhere they want at any time. There are so many kids out there now that I don't think they'll ever get them off the street."

"We probably had a lot more flexibility back then than officers do now," adds Norma Wilson. "There was a curfew law and that gave us an excuse to stop kids on the street and inquire about how old they were and why they were out late. That was our way of keeping track of who was out on the streets at night. We usually called their homes to find out if they had permission to be out, and to see if their parents knew where their kids were. And we had the right to ask parents, 'What are your kids doing out on the street?' We had the right to do it even though we had no evidence the kids were involved in a particular crime."

In addition to the curfew laws, the women also had the aid of City Ordinance 160146, which broadly outlawed "contributing to the delinquency" and "dependency of a minor." The law was so broad it was used for a variety of offenses, including drinking in public.

"That was the catchall, and we arrested parents under that ordinance," Robinson explains. "I think sometimes it's too bad we don't still have it because if you charged the parents with a criminal charge, even a misdemeanor, it seemed to get their attention for at least a period of time. They didn't want to go to jail."

To oversee the welfare of lost and mistreated children, the policewomen drove around the city in unmarked cars and frequently went to some of the seediest areas of the city. Often, the women were out alone.

"We were often at a lot of risk because we didn't have the backup support that patrol officers had," Skagen notes. "Most of the time we were making calls and going into places where there was a high threat, and we were there on our own. We didn't log in and log out every car in the Women's Bureau at that time, so dispatch didn't always know where our investigation took us. We had an address and we'd go there looking for runaways and often find ourselves in some very hostile, criminal environments.

"It was not unusual for us to be drawing our guns. We were often in the worst parts of town looking for runaways. At that time, it was a violation of the law for kids to run away from home, and we could take them into custody. I once took on this drunk teenager. I told her she was under arrest and she said she had to go to the bathroom first. We went in and she started fighting with me. She was a lot bigger than I was, and the first thing she said was, 'Do you know karate?' I said, 'I sure do.' I didn't, but saying I did helped make her hesitate. Still, she got pretty wild. I got her under control, but my shoulder was dislocated in the process.

"One time I was looking for a runaway in an empty house," she adds. "I was up on the porch all by myself and nobody was around, the house was empty, and I thought I would just peer inside the windows to see what I could see. Suddenly two cars pulled up, and these guys got out and surrounded me. They were very abusive and I could tell they were dangerous people. So I just bluffed my way through. I told them police detectives were on the way and that they'd better get out of there before the detectives arrived. Fortunately they decided I was telling the truth and got out of there. Boy, later I got chewed out by my sergeant for that misadventure!"

Despite operating in dangerous neighborhoods, the policewomen of the late fifties had one extra factor in their favor—citizens generally respected the police.

"In those days, you felt that if you put your badge out there, that little badge was going to protect you from anything," notes Beryl Thompson. "In some ways, I think people listened to us more. I can remember really chewing people out and telling them that I was going to be back the next day, and that I wanted the place cleaned up and the children bathed. Nine times out of ten they did it. Nowadays, you would just have the door slammed in your face. The level of respect was so much higher."

"It wasn't that we were social workers all the time," Karas says, in retrospect. "We made drunk-driving arrests, tracked down stolen cars, and went undercover on sex cases. We were also called out on drug deals, handled female prisoners in court, helped with certain probation matters, stood by on parade routes, and provided security by circling the stage for celebrities like Elvis when they came to town.

"Every day was a new day," she reflects. "You never knew what was going to happen and that was what I liked about the job. And I enjoyed seventy-five percent of the officers I worked with because they were neat fellows. In those days you'd go out on a case with a fellow and maybe you worked it up, maybe he worked it up, but you'd go together. And if you made a really good arrest, and everything went fine, he'd come back in, put his arm around you, give you a hug and say, 'Hey, Karas, you did good.' I mean, think of what would happen today—the guy would probably get written up for sexual harassment because he hugged a woman officer. In our day, I think we enjoyed a great sense of camaraderie, and an *esprit de corps.*"

3

NOSES POWDERED AND READY FOR DUTY

"Four new members of the Police Department's patrol division powdered their noses this morning and reported for duty.

The new "patrolmen" are policewomen transferred from the Women's Bureau to the patrol division, marking the first time Seattle policewomen have been used for such duties."

-*The Seattle Times*, March 23, 1961

As with all things American, the 1960s proved to be a revolutionary decade for policewomen nationwide. While the efforts of Dr. Martin Luther King, Jr. and other black leaders were forging a civil rights revolution for African Americans, New York City policewomen were battling a different form of segregation by filing a lawsuit to force the NYPD to allow them to test for promotions to sergeant alongside men. When their legal challenge succeeded, departments across the country began to desegregate their police forces. Seattle was no exception, and by the end of the decade the Women's Bureau would be officially disbanded.

Such changes were still years away, however, when the SPD officials announced in 1961 that they would launch a "bold experiment" to see if women could serve as "all-purpose police officers." To accomplish this, policewomen were officially transferred to the Patrol Division for three-month stints in regular patrols on the streets and in city parks. They were also assigned to work as decoys in neighborhoods where women had been targeted by criminals, and for surveillance work where female cops would be less obtrusive than men. "Of course," patrol division Chief Charles A. Rouse declared to the press, "we wouldn't have them walking a skid row beat at night."

Although Sylvia Hunsicker had walked such a beat back in the 1920s, the early 1960s experiment was designed to be tamer. In the days of Andy of Mayberry, Ozzie and Harriett, and the father who knew best, few Americans thought of women in the role of law enforcer. Certainly, the average citizen was not expecting to be pulled over by a patrol car and have a skirt-wearing policewoman step out to write them the ticket.

"The response we got from the public was really funny," Mary Robinson says. "People would drive down the street and suddenly look over and see these uniformed women in a bubble car. We were always getting double-takes, and on many occasions almost caused accidents."

"Joyce Johnson and I were supposed to get some 'movers' — traffic violators," Karen Ejde recalls, "so we asked some of our pals in our squad where to find good duck ponds, places where you can just sit and pick them off. Up on Broadway at John Street there was a good one, because you couldn't turn left at that intersection. We parked up there and we didn't have to wait long before someone made an illegal turn in front of us. Joyce and I took turns driving and writing the tickets. On one of our first stops, Joyce got out and she was flustered, the poor thing, because she had never made a traffic stop before. She had to ask the male driver what kind of car he drove, forgot what the violation was for, and cited him for something else. The bad thing was he was a university professor of sociology or something, and we later learned that he used that stop as an example in his lectures about the ineptness of some people in authority."

"The men I stopped would laugh," Helen Karas notes. "They'd think it was a big joke, sign their ticket and go home and tell their wives that some broad had pulled them over. But every woman I stopped—what bitches they were. They were constantly denying they did anything wrong. They'd say, 'I wasn't and you know I wasn't' or, 'Don't you have anything better to do?' And they were nasty, really nasty. They just didn't like the idea of a sister giving them a ticket, especially a ticket they were certain they didn't deserve. I had a very short fuse, and I had to practically stand on my toe so I wouldn't say anything I'd later regret. I'd always smile and say, 'Now, I hope you will drive a little slower in the future.' The nasty ones would reply, 'Oh, shit, you bitch,' or something like that. I'd just keep smiling and say, 'To each her own,' and walk off."

"I think for some women, it was embarrassing," Ejde adds. "They didn't know how they were going to explain this to their husband."

For many policewomen, the "bold experiment" to place them into patrol was interesting but ill-designed.

"We weren't really dressed appropriately for the job," Beryl Thompson notes. "Rather than wearing slacks so we could get down on the ground and run fast over any terrain, we were still dressed in a skirt and jacket. And instead of wearing a gun belt we had our guns in a purse on a shoulder strap, and that was impractical. If we got into a tussle with somebody that purse would come off really easily. I think it was very dangerous."

While male officers were assigned to squads that worked specific districts in the city, the policewomen were frequently assigned to umbrella cars at night and were on call citywide. Most nights they were at the mercy of male radio operators who, more often than not, enjoyed sending them every which way on any number of possible crimes.

"We could be sent to anything," Thompson says, "but we only had the one car for the entire city and we were dispatched out of the central downtown precinct. So if male patrol officers had a rape case they wanted to assign to us or they needed a policewoman for any reason, we got the call regardless of where it was. One dispatcher thought it would be cute to give the women an accident on the viaduct during rush hour even though we were roaming the entire city and there were closer cars. Also, I think we probably got more of the late calls just before shift change so we'd be tied up doing paperwork after we were supposed to be off."

"I was working the night shift, had a gal partner, and the fellow in radio dispatch had been in my academy class," Karas adds. "What does he do? One night at about 9 p.m. we were called up to an attempted burglary up on First Hill near downtown. We finished up with that and then he called us to go uptown to 143rd in the north end to investigate an attempted poisoning of a dog. Then I was on my way back downtown and he tried to send me somewhere else. I said, 'I have to take this evidence in.' 'What evidence?' 'The poisoned bone.' I almost said something else, but I didn't. I got back on the air eventually and was sent out to the north end again on another stupid inane call. We were jacked around all over the place.

"Finally, one night I reached my limit. After being sent this way and that, I drove back to the station, went up to the radio room and I screamed at him, 'You sonofabitch! If you do this to me another night, you're not going to live through it!' I was so mad I was just purple, and I really lost it completely. Unfortunately, there were a number of people who heard me. But I never got called on the carpet, and from that day forward the calls were at least halfway decent."

Besides being at the mercy of overly playful radio operators, the policewomen also encountered patrol officers who were less than happy to have the women on their beats.

"One night we were sent up on Queen Anne Hill to investigate a burglary," Karas explains. "The burglars had come through the roof of this fellow's apartment, and we were taking down all of the information. My partner was wondering how in the hell we were going to get up on the roof wearing our skirts. About that time two male officers came in and said, 'What in the hell are you doing in our district?'

"Well, of course we'd been sent there by dispatch, and the male officers knew that because they could hear us being sent over the radio. But they came fumbling over there to give us the wherewithal, and I realized we were going to have a knockdown fight. You can't do that in front of a citizen so I just said, 'Oh, nice of you boys to show up.' I told them what we'd done, and then we went on our way. If I'd told them what was really on my mind, I would have said, 'Who do you SOBs think you are? We received the call, you didn't, so what are *you* doing here?'

"We experienced this kind of attitude from some of the men," she adds. "So, what did we do? We figured out a little way to get even with them. On First Avenue between 12 and 4 a.m., parking was illegal because that was the time the streets were cleaned. In those days, there were officers who were very partial to some of the bars on First Avenue and we knew they frequently parked down on the street between 12 and 4 a.m. One night we went down in our car, parked behind them and wrote tickets on their cars. We wrote about twenty tickets, and pretty soon we got called into our sergeant's office. He asked us, 'How come you're writing tickets?' I said, 'Parking on First at that time of night is against the law, and we were told to get active and do more traffic enforcement. These are good, solid tickets, and how better to make money? This is a cinch.'

"'Well you can't do that,' the sergeant told us. I said, 'Well, now, somebody's breaking the law right in front of me and I can't write them a ticket?' He didn't really have an answer to that so we kept on writing tickets. Then the officers started watching for us. When they saw us coming some would come out and jump into their cars. So we started parking our car a few blocks down and walked up to write the tickets. We were on a lot of people's list for quite a while because of that."

Going out on patrol gave the women insight into many aspects of police work that they had not experienced before, including the realization that some male officers were involved in more illegal activities than just parking in a no-parking zone.

"I was single, I was buying a house, and I drove a car my folks had given me," Karas recalls. "My house payments were thirty-five dollars a month, and I had to pay insurance on the car and on the house. I managed to get by on my salary but I wasn't putting a lot of money in the bank. But there were fellows who were married, had several kids, a pick-up truck, a boat, some property somewhere else, and they seemed to be able to go to Hawaii once in a while with the wife and kids. I wondered how they were doing it because I was getting the same pay they were.

"We used to go down to a restaurant in Chinatown, and the owners put on a free dinner for all the officers. They were serving straight whiskey out of glasses, not a little shot glass, and I couldn't understand. I thought, *Gees, they're doing this because they love policemen.* I was smart, but I didn't initially think about crooked cops. Then it came out that the officers were going in there on duty, having a drink or two, and I learned the truth—they were on the take.

"At the time I was going out with a merchant marine," she adds. "He had come to town and he had about six hundred dollars in his pocket that he was planning to put in the bank. He got stopped by some officers and was arrested for being drunk even though he'd only had a few beers. He told me that when he was being put into the paddy wagon he got rolled for the six hundred bucks. I couldn't believe it, and I told him, 'No way, our officers wouldn't do that.'

"Then one night I came in off of patrol, and I was sitting in my car while my partner took an arrest report into the station. Here comes the paddy wagon. Two officers, one of them was the current husband of the captain of the Women's Bureau, got out and opened up the back to take out a suspect. I sat there and watched the two officers as they took the guy's wallet and relieved it of some cash. They shook him down and didn't know I was sitting there watching. So what do you do? Who do you tell? You don't tell. That's the code of silence. If you want to keep working where you are, and you don't want a hassle, you forget about it. The guy was being brought in drunk and they cleaned out his wallet before he went into the booking office. Whoever was in the booking office probably got their share too. There were definitely officers on the take, but fortunately they were the minority."

"Over the years I suspected a lot of things," Norma Wilson recalls. "You can't be around the precinct without thinking of it, but a lot of the guys were very nice to me. There wasn't anything I knew personally, but the gals in jail would tell me a lot of things. They would say that some of officers would beat them up, or that some of the prostitutes would have to service the men. I said, 'If you want to sign a complaint, I'll take the statement and see that it gets to the right person.' But none of them ever would.

"The men also used to give homosexuals a hard time, especially the ones who were made up like women. There were a lot of nightclubs downtown on First Avenue in those days that had female impersonators, and some of them were really good looking. Every once in a while, they would get thrown in jail, and they would tell me stories about how the male officers beat them up. Again, they would never file a complaint."

Ultimately, and with no fanfare, the experiment of putting policewomen in patrol was deemed to be unsuccessful and the women went back to full-time work in the Women's Bureau. To many of the policewomen, the experiment was designed to fail from the start.

"We were used poorly most of the time," Karas explains. "It wasn't that we couldn't have gone out on patrol as a regular job, but we weren't originally hired for patrol and by the time they wanted to start this patrol bit, we were all aging."

"More important than the age factor was the lack of training," adds Karen Ejde. "When we went to the police academy it was a lot different than it is now. We were not trained for high-speed chases or to work traffic stops. I didn't dislike patrol *per se*, but the overall feeling was that we were not really earning our keep there. We were not being utilized to the best possible advantage. We were supposed to be an umbrella car that was at the disposal of the patrol division during the swing shift, and there were times when we helped out in significant ways. But the whole scheme of things was not well thought out. My resentment about being in patrol in the early 1960s was it was a waste of my time, my skills, and my training. I felt we were being misused to prove something to somebody. It could have been that the brass was under pressure from City Hall across the street. I don't know, but it was a bit insulting."

"It is true that they didn't know what they were doing with us out there," offers Jean Selvidge Dunbar. "At the same time, I think a lot of policewomen resented it and would not accept that this was a new thing. They wanted to do more of the social work, and did not want to be out there giving traffic tickets. I think in some ways it was a good use of the women, and in some ways it was a waste. Frankly, we turned out to be primarily glorified clerks. If the patrol clerk had a night off, they would use the policewomen on that shift to be the patrol clerk and we'd end up doing all the paperwork."

"I thought they were just trying to appease the political leaders who thought it was time to show off some women in uniform," Wilson adds. "One of the other things we did in uniform was work the presidential detail when President Kennedy came to Seattle. We went down in uniform, men and women both, and stood around the Olympic Hotel when he came through with his Secret Service entourage. I'm not quite sure why they wanted a bunch of uniformed women and men in the lobby, but I remember they said, 'It's important that you stand still, you don't move, you don't do this, you don't do that.' By the end of the day, my body was just aching from standing still. It's the hardest thing to do. But I did get to see President Kennedy up close because he walked right by us."

While the women were pulled from the umbrella car and patrol assignments, they continued to experience expanded duties. Many weekends found them working crowd control at football games and rock concerts, where they encountered an increasingly hostile public.

"I got injured at the first Beatles concert," Noreen Skagen recalls. "There were about four of us trying to keep the kids under control, and I was assigned to the first aid room. The kids were absolutely out of control, absolutely hysterical. Then the lights went out in the auditorium and they panicked. The next day I had bruises on my feet, my legs, my arms, and my back. It was just wild."

The policewomen also encountered protesters upset with the war, the government, and other ills. The women endured being spat on and being called names. However, by department directive, all the Seattle Police Department officers were ordered to hold their tongues.

"They sent a list around the department of all the names we couldn't use," Karas notes with a laugh. "They weren't necessarily dirty names or bad names, but they were considered inflammatory and unprofessional, and could be misinterpreted as being uncomplimentary. There were thirty-two of these names. So the kids would come up to us and call us an SOB and motherfucker, and I would turn to another officer and say, 'Well what do you think? Do you think that was number 2 on the list, 22, or 24?' We'd laugh so hard, it took our tension down."

Many aspects of the Women's Bureau were different in the sixties, not the least of which was the command staff. After a thirty-five-year career, Irene Durham retired from the SPD in 1956. Sergeant Kay Twohig was promoted to captain and became the last female commander of the Women's Bureau.

Captain Twohig proved to be a marked departure from the more administration-oriented Captain Durham. Where Durham left the day-to-day running of her bureau to Mrs. Elliott, Twohig tried to be more hands-on, and it was a shift many policewomen found difficult to accept.

"Captain Twohig insisted on going out with us on patrol one night," Karas recalls. "We went into the Unique Grill on First Avenue. It was one of the favorite hangouts of runaways and bad kids. The owner and his wife were good friends of ours and if they saw something suspicious they'd give us a call. I don't think the kids ever realized that was why we showed up a number of times. Many of the kids were runaways or juvenile delinquents, and you had to approach them carefully. You had to go in to a place quietly, and maybe sit and have a cup of coffee. Sometimes a kid or two would come over and talk to us, and we'd say, 'Okay fellows, well you know I'm the police, and I have to know who you are because of the hour of the night. So why don't we talk a little bit.' It all had to happen real easy.

"Well, when the Captain came with us, she decided she wanted to handle some kids who were there. But she didn't know how to talk to people, and she got the kids incensed. The Captain was brash and a little bit impressed with her position. She asked the kids very blunt questions, and you don't approach kids that way, especially juvenile runaways. You don't go in and say, 'Hey, I'm Karas and see my badge and what are you kids doing here?' That would turn kids off."

"It is awkward and a little unpleasant to talk about somebody who is deceased and can't defend herself, but that is the truth," adds Ejde. "Captain Twohig was not blessed with a manner of great tact and human understanding."

"She would interfere and get into your cases," notes Norma Wilson, more bluntly. "She'd know what you'd done because you'd usually write notes in the file, and then she would call up your contacts and insist that they come down or tell them to do certain things I wouldn't have. Then she wouldn't write anything down. She'd put the file back in the folder and I'd never know a thing about it until it backfired. She used to make appointments for me and not tell me about them. Then, when I would come in from doing other things, these people would be waiting for me and they would just be boiling mad because they thought I had called them into the station."

Perhaps more disturbing to the women was Captain's Twohig's interference in their personal lives.

"She called us 'her girls,' " Karas explains, "and we didn't like that at all. She would provide dates for you, or she'd bring an out-of-town fellow in and tell you to take him to lunch. Well, who the hell wants to take somebody to lunch you'd never met before? Plus, most of the men she set us up with were at the lower end of the totem pole, guys we would never have considered being caught dead with. Let me tell you, she was something else."

"We used to have a policeman's ball and the guys would come down from Vancouver, Canada," Wilson adds. "Captain Twohig liked to buddy with them and have drinks with them, and then she'd make dates for us with the unmarried guys without telling us. The guys would just show up at the station and say, 'Well, do you want to go out and have a drink now?' I'd say, 'Who are you?' It was hard working for Kay, there's just no question about it."

While Captain Twohig's efforts to set her "girls" up were not successful, many of policewomen did date men on the department. For some, like Skagen, Wilson and Dunbar, dating cops eventually led to marriage. For others, it remained a side benefit of the job.

"I dated men on the department," Karas recalls. "I had fun with a lot of them, and also got into trouble with lots of them. Some of them dated you, and then later you found out they were married. That wasn't very pleasant.

"I also went out with men who did not do police work," she adds. "The problem with dating guys who weren't policemen was they didn't understand our jobs. I had one male friend I was very fond of. He had a regular job that gave him Saturday and Sunday off. We would plan for dinner say on a Thursday, and then I would be sent on a stake out. I couldn't call because he wouldn't be home and there were no message machines in those days. Well, how many times does a fellow take this before he says, 'Sayonara'? He'd say, 'Get a decent job.' "

As the 1960s rolled on, the work of the Women's Bureau continued to change. New women coming on the scene in the mid- to late sixties found themselves going out on unusual and even dangerous undercover assignments while still in the academy. Among the newcomers were Pat Lamphere and Marilyn McLaughlin. For Lamphere, becoming a policewoman in 1967 represented a dream come true because she was continuing a family tradition.

"My dad was a cop in Tacoma, Washington," Lamphere explains, "and I wanted to be a policewoman because I just adored him. He was a wonderful man and I considered him to be a role model. The fact that he was a man and I was a woman made no difference. He never encouraged me to be a police officer, but I think he was very proud.

"He wasn't an old-style cop because he was faithful to his wife and family, and he wasn't on the take," she adds. "I learned that after I went on the Seattle Police Department and I was working nights. I just couldn't believe the men. Most of them were married and they were still asking you out. They were unbelievable. I got off work one night shift, drove to Tacoma, got my dad out of bed at one or two in the morning, and said, 'What is it with these guys?' Because my dad always came home. He might have worked nights, but he was always at home at the times he wasn't working. And my dad was real straight. I mean, in the 1940s, cops didn't make any money and many Tacoma police were on the take. But we were poor."

Although Lamphere's career path seems obvious now, back when she graduated from high school she considered a very different vocation—being a nun.

"I went into a convent out of high school, and stayed about one year. I was very Catholic. The nuns were terrific and my folks thought it was great. But it was still very restrictive. It was a semi-cloistered order and you really cut yourself off from your family.

"I was just about to take my first vows as a novitiate when I decided it was not for me and left the convent. I think if it had been a little more relaxed like it became even five years later, I'd probably still be there."

Lamphere opted to go to Washington State University where she majored in social work. After graduation, she wanted to become a police officer, but the Women's Bureau and its equivalent in nearby Tacoma were not hiring. However, after a brief stint working in juvenile court, she was allowed to test with the SPD and was hired when the Bureau suddenly expanded its ranks. Once appointed, Lamphere immediately went to the police academy where she soon realized women were not always treated equally.

"We really weren't equals in the academy," she explains. "They wouldn't let us do the pursuit driving like the men were doing. We had to stay in the office and do office work. That incensed me. We also didn't have to shoot the shotgun. I said, 'You mean, I'm going to be around this thing and I'm not going to learn how to shoot it? I am going to shoot a shotgun.' And I did. We also had to wear these silly seersucker-type skirts and jackets, and we had these little teeny .32 pistols, and little teeny badges. Even so, I never thought I wasn't the men's equal—it was just that I was hired to do a different job."

Despite the inequities, Lamphere had a great time training with her male counterparts.

"I liked everything about the academy," she notes. "The information was great, I learned a lot of stuff, and there was a wonderful camaraderie among the class. Our class was really social and we had a lot of parties and get-togethers. We also took swimming in those days. The other two ladies weren't good swimmers but I was, and I was the only lady who went into the lifesaving part. That was a hoot. We were all up at the YMCA pool. The guys were huge, and they were the ones you had to rescue. I'd practically go down trying to save them. I also loved the academy because the other female cadets were all married. I was the only single woman, and it was great. The men were fabulous. I ended up dating two of them."

Once she completed the academy, Lamphere found herself blazing new ground as a policewoman. Instead of being given a normal Women's Bureau caseload, she was immediately assigned to work undercover for the Vice Squad.

"They started a prostitute program where we walked the street," Lamphere says. "We were one of the first cities in the nation to do that. The Vice Squad asked only those women who were not married and, because I was so young—I was twenty-three at the time—I was always asked to go undercover. When somebody found out that I had been in the convent and then was walking the streets for the police department they wrote this big article. They thought it was such a hoot. They had this big picture of me on the front page of *The Seattle Post-Intelligencer* with me in a shadow with a cigarette, and I had on this short, short skirt that showed my legs. It was really funny. My dad looked at the photo and said, 'I don't believe those look like your legs. Who is that?'

"Working the prostitution unit was pretty scary for a new recruit," she recalls, "and the guys all laughed because I was so naïve. I was working with the old vice squad, and half of these guys were the ones who were later arrested at the end of the 1960s for having been on the take for many years. They didn't know how to deal with me. I didn't know anything, so I would go to them and say, 'You guys have got to tell me what some of these terms are. I don't know what an "around the world" is. You've got to start explaining this stuff to me so I'll know what to charge.' We started the undercover in Chinatown, and they always had to buy me a stiff drink at the beginning of my shift because I had to have one before I could walk the streets."

Lamphere also went on drug busts involving defendants who were among the most dangerous in the city.

"The only truly scary instance I had during the whole twenty-seven years I was on the police department," Lamphere notes, "was when Officer Bob Holder and I were acting like a couple to try to get into a suspected drug house in the north end. We didn't want to have to break the door in because we'd heard they had firearms inside and that they had the door really secure. So Bob and I acted like a couple trying to buy dope.

"We walked up to the front of the house and knocked. This guy came to the door with a gun in one hand and a baby in the other. The guy didn't know who we were, and he got anxious because he thought we were there to rip him off. He pointed his gun directly at Bob and me. The way we got out of it was Bob started telling him that we actually were the police. The guy had us at the door for what seemed like forever, but I'm sure it was really only a matter of seconds. Then he put his gun down and let us in. Back then, once they knew we were the police, they were pretty much respectful of us.

"Bob Holder was a really with-it guy," Lamphere adds. "He was a funny man who sometimes had a mouth that didn't quit. We were serving a warrant one day, and some young guy was real foul-mouthed. Holder said, 'Stop using language like that. Don't talk like that in front of a lady.' The guy said a whole bunch more words. Holder picked him up, took him into another room and shut him in there. We got back to the office and I said, 'Holder, I've heard you guys all say a lot worse words right in front of me.' He said, 'Yeah, but we know you and respect you.' "

Besides undercover stings, Lamphere and the other policewomen in the sixties were used in a variety of ways to investigate drug-related crimes.

"The female suspects always carried the drugs up their wahoos so we policewomen always went along to do searches," Lamphere explains. "That was my first introduction to having a woman bend over and spread her cheeks so I could shine a flashlight *up there*. We had to do it a lot because they all carried their drugs up there—or as one of the old-time narcotics guys referred to it—up in their paisley purse.

"We got loaned out every so often to the narcotics unit and it was always heroin we were going after," Karas adds. "In those days, I'd go to the door and say, 'Avon calling' or something, and there would be officers ready at the back door. Federal officers would also often go with us. Once the door was open, I would step aside and the guys would go right past me and towards the john. They usually knew the location of the illegal drugs because they had people in there who were buying undercover. We would go through the house with a fine-toothed comb. We'd take the diapers off the kids, and often times the drugs would be stuffed in there. We'd also go into the kitchen, take out the sugar can, dump it on the floor, take out the coffee can, dump it on top of the sugar, then take the flour, dump it on top of the coffee. When we got all through searching, we left the house in total disrepair. Nowadays officers and detectives take a picture when they go in and they take a picture when they go out because it has to look the same way. But I think it made more of an impact on the individuals in the house the way we did it."

In addition to drug busts and prostitution undercovers, the policewomen also found themselves prowling in the most unlikely of places.

"While the guys got to arrest hookers downtown, we girls had our own duty called the Dirty Man Details at the downtown public library," explains Marlynn McLaughlin, who joined the department in 1969. "The library was having problems with perverts—men exposing themselves, molesting children, and molesting women in the elevators, the restrooms and behind the book stacks. This all sounded pretty absurd to us because the downtown library was a modern building with fairly open spaces, at least where the books were kept.

"We were sent down there to prowl the stacks and see what action we could find. Believe me, it didn't take much to get some action. You would be standing there reading a book and the next thing you knew, some guy wearing a suit was sliding in between your legs. We had teams of men watching for this and as soon as something happened, they would come out from behind the stacks and nab the guy. It was just incredible."

The Dirty Man Detail continued for several months, with mostly positive results. "At one of the staff meetings regarding our progress, the library staff made a presentation to the policewoman running the detail," McLaughlin recalls. "They gave her a little package, and inside she found a pair of lady's panties. Written on the crotch in black felt tip was 'You're under arrest.' Try to do that nowadays and I'm sure somebody would have a fit, but we just cracked up."

While the Dirty Man Detail had its surprises, not all the undercover work was as humorous or as safe.

"Back before *Roe v. Wade* made abortions legal, I was sent out as a decoy on an illegal abortion sting," McLaughlin says. "The abortionist was a butcher by trade who had learned his technique in Hawaii, and he used a catheter, a rubber hose, a wire coat hanger, and a bottle of antibacterial disinfectant. He charged $100 with a money-back guarantee."

The Vice Squad learned about the man's activities after a young student almost died from one of his "guaranteed" operations. With the student's teacher acting as a go-between, McLaughlin was set up as a decoy student who needed an abortion. The teacher arranged to meet the butcher at a bowling alley, and the plan was to go to a motel, get the man to agree to take money for the procedure, and then give the signal to detectives to come in and arrest him. However, nothing went as planned.

"We met the butcher at the bowling alley," McLaughlin explains, "but soon after we got into our car, he directed us away from the motel and we lost our tail car. The man directed us to a pornographic photography studio located underneath a freeway. Fortunately, the teacher kept her cool. She started driving real slowly and when we got to the parking lot she kept tapping the brakes, flashing the brake lights so the detectives would hopefully spot us.

The tail car caught up to their car pulling into the parking lot. McLaughlin and the teacher went into the photography studio with the abortionist. Once inside, he locked the front door, and escorted the women into a backroom where the abortion was going to take place.

"We talked about how he was going to do the procedure, and I tried to get him to take the money," the policewoman says. "But the man didn't immediately accept. Meanwhile, the detectives outside got nervous and knocked on the front door. The suspect rushed into the front room and pulled a rifle on them just as they came through the door. After a brief standoff, the man agreed to drop his rifle.

"They arrested him, and I was just shaking. I mean, I was not even out of the academy yet, and I hadn't been an officer long enough to feel that I had control of anything. Plus, I had no weapon on me or any way to protect the teacher or myself. But that was the way Vice wanted to do it, and they got hell for that later. After the arrest, the detectives took me out to a bar and poured a couple of drinks into me.

"I still remember a moment when we were in the backroom with the butcher before the detectives came in," McLaughlin adds with a chill in her voice. "The suspect brought out a camera case which he opened, and inside was a coat hanger with rust on it that he was going to use to do the operation. How could anyone do that to another human being? I definitely think that abortions should be legal because if they aren't, if that right is taken away, you'll have people like him doing the procedure. Nobody should ever be subjected to that."

4

UPWARDLY MOBILE... AT LAST

During the late 1960s when all the marches were going on, the policewomen were on standby for what they called 'UOs' — Unusual Occurrences. Instead of going out on the street during those events, we were assigned to work on booking teams. The male officers would bring the bad guys in to be photographed, and then we would sit at our typewriters and type the reports as the men explained why they'd made the arrest. It was so funny because back then if the prisoners used foul language, we were supposed to type it into the report. The male officers would be hesitant to say the foul language in front of us because they weren't brought up to swear in front of women. We had to tell them, "You've got to say it and you've got to spell it because we've got to get it into the report. "
— Officer Marlynn McLaughlin

The idea that women couldn't handle the harsh realities of the street, let alone foul language, was ingrained in the white male police establishment of the late 1960s. But times were changing and the men were soon forced to accept women in roles they never dreamed, from working side-by-side in the same units to having a female commanding officer.

"It was a long time coming, but for many years we didn't have the guts to step forward and knock on the door," says Beryl Thompson. "On the one hand, you knew what the job was when you took it, so you couldn't complain. On the other hand, after you had been there a while and you saw men get promoted above you who went through the academy with you, were no smarter than you, and were no better at what they were doing—some less so—it started to get frustrating. Suddenly you saw your job as looking more like a dead-end than their jobs and the only reason was because they were men and you were a woman."

The change in Seattle occurred in part because in 1961 New York City Policewoman Felicia Shpritzer launched a successful court fight for the right to test for promotions alongside her male counterparts. However, while the suit's outcome was enough to set into motion the end of segregation on police departments nationwide, the Seattle Police Department in 1968 was also rocked by scandal when several male vice detectives were discovered to be on the take. In the turmoil that followed this revelation, the chief of police resigned, and the Seattle Police Department commissioned a study of its departmental structure by the International Association of Chiefs of Police. Among the commission's many recommendations was the call to disband the Women's Bureau and to assign the policewomen to regular positions throughout the department. The SPD followed the recommendation. As a result, Marlynn McLaughlin was the last woman hired under the Women's Bureau banner, and the last to be hired as a "policewoman."

"On the day of the announcement the entire Women's Bureau—or everyone who was working that day—was herded into a room," Thompson recalls. "The chief and the director of personnel started talking to us about the fact that, 'Well, you are going to be able to take promotions, but first we have to decide what jobs you can work.' It was prefaced by saying, 'Well, do you really want to do this? We had our own career plan for you'—unspoken of course—'and if you decide to go through with this, we can't select you out and put you in an easier job, a less dangerous or less stressful job. You're going to have to be able to do any job, even ride motorcycles, and how would you feel about having to lift up a 250-pound motorcycle?' "

"Everybody in the room laughed of course," adds Pat Lamphere. "George Tiltsch was the chief at the time, and he made it sound like this big deal, like we were all doomed because he was going to have to put us in places that he just knew we didn't want to be. Beryl Thompson thought it was a lot more appalling than I did at the time. I had to have more living experience before I would know. I think he really believed women weren't going to be able to compete equally for this job, and we weren't going to be able to do it. Of course, in those days everybody thought that to be a female patrol officer, you had to do the job like a man. And the women believed that too. The guy was really putting us down, but we held our tongues."

"No woman challenged the department at that point," Thompson notes. "We were a product of the times, of our upbringing and our education. And that was how women were treated in all professions at that time, not just in the police department."

Despite the prediction of utter doom, the SPD moved forward with the dismantling of the Women's Bureau and assigned the policewomen to detective positions throughout the department. Yet, the moves were not done with complete equality in mind. For example, while the women now suddenly worked side-by-side with male detectives and had the same caseloads, they were not given the rank and salary their male counterparts enjoyed; instead, they retained the title of Policewomen and were paid the same as less senior patrol officers. Similarly, four policewomen who had handled female juveniles in the Women's Bureau kept their same positions in a new, gender-neutral Juvenile Unit, but newly assigned male detectives were allowed to take over the desks already in use by the women.

The women transferred into Juvenile were doing a job they were very familiar with, and their new commander at least understood and recognized their qualifications. Policewomen who were transferred to other bureaus, however, frequently encountered male commanding officers who had no idea how to deal with females in their units.

"Karen Ejde and I requested to transfer to the detectives unit handling illegal bank checks and forgery," Helen Karas notes. "After we were granted our request we were told to report to the division. The deputy chief came in and welcomed us. He was a likeable guy and although he was always very pleasant, he did not know how to address us. I think he tried to convey a friendly welcome, but it was obvious that he didn't really believe we had much to add to his unit. He concluded his brief talk by saying, 'Well, I don't know exactly what you're going to be doing up here but, if nothing else, just hang around, look cute, and keep the coffee on.' "

Karas found the captain to be particularly challenging because he had a rather different view of what was important. Once, when a rare snowstorm paralyzed Seattle streets and effectively brought the city to a halt, Karas and Ejde managed to walk through the blizzard and showed up to work wearing pants. While none of the other detectives made it into work that day, the captain took the women to task because they weren't wearing their assigned policewomen uniform of skirts and high heels.

Many years later, Karas encountered the captain and was surprised to hear how fond he was of her.

"At a reunion dinner the captain told me, 'You know, Helen, I really had to play politics to get you two girls in my unit. I wanted you there and I really had to pull some strings to get you.' And I thought, *It sounds like he'd purchased two bodies.* Women were still property. It's hard to relate to somebody like that. I shouldn't say this at this late date but I had very little respect for him. To me he was the epitome of how some men felt about women."

"When I was assigned to the criminal investigations unit as a detective, I got the 'morals lecture,' " adds Marlynn McLaughlin with a laugh. "That's where you're told how to act as a detective. I thought it was pretty interesting. The head of criminal investigations had us come into his office. He then lectured a young male officer and myself on how we should conduct ourselves. He said, 'You are police officers. You have to be aware that people will be looking at your behavior on and off duty, so you have to be one step above.' About two weeks later, he asked me out for drinks after work. I was married and he was married too, so there you go."

Although the top brass was uncertain of how to best use the policewomen, most rank-and-file detectives accepted the females with little resistance.

"The men reacted with anxiety to a certain extent," Noreen Skagen offers, "but I think they mostly thought it was fair to let us move throughout the department. By that point, we were well known. We had done a lot of work for them, and we'd taken a lot of work off their shoulders that they didn't want to do. So there were not a lot of problems with the men at that time, and I think many of them welcomed the change. Even so, at first we were only offered certain types of cases. Gradually, after we'd settled into the units, we started doing all kinds of cases and there was no longer a separation of caseload."

While the other policewomen were assigned to detective units, Beryl Thompson found herself temporarily assigned to patrol. Unlike her experiences in the early 1960s, this assignment involved working for a squad in the North Precinct and driving regular car assignments. Being the first woman assigned to that precinct created unique challenges. One was merely practical—there was no separate changing area for her, so she had to use one of the interview rooms to change into her uniform if it wasn't occupied. Others involved the response she received from the older generation of patrol officers.

"The younger men expected you to carry your weight," Thompson explains, "but the old-timers were more resistant. One officer saw a posting that we were going to be together in a two-person car the following day, and he went to the sergeant and told him he wouldn't ride with me. I was called in off the street, and the whole squad was called back by the sergeant. We went to the roll call room, and I had to sit up there with the sergeant and defend myself. I got through it okay, but it was a bit uncomfortable to sit up there and answer the questions of your coworkers about your ability to do the work. Then I was given the opportunity to say a few words. I told them that I was there to do the job, and I would do it. At that point, most of the men backed down, including the guy who had refused to ride with me."

When Thompson first showed up at the North Precinct, she was wearing the traditional policewoman's skirt, jacket, and heels. That quickly changed when it proved impractical.

"I talked with the precinct captain and said, 'This just isn't going to work,' " Thompson recalls. "I requested that I wear slacks and a regular police shirt. He went along with that. That was unique because none of the other policewomen were doing that."

After her stint in patrol, Thompson found herself cycled for a brief time through the Homicide and Robbery Unit.

"The reception again was perhaps somewhat mixed, but overall it was very supportive. I would say more so from the detectives than from the sergeants. I do recall I was given one case where I wanted to make an arrest, and I felt the easiest way to do that was to take the suspect at work. I made arrangements with the company the suspect worked for and then went to the sergeant to ask for someone else from the squad to go with me. His response was, 'Well, after you get out there, call patrol if you need any help.'

"His denial of my request was ridiculous, especially when the men in the division were going out practically hand-in-hand in pairs on all their cases. But I didn't argue with the sergeant— back then I don't think any of us would have. I went out to the company and, as it turned out, the arrest went without incident. I did call patrol after I arrested the man, and they came out and helped me with the transport. But it could have been a dangerous situation, and you just didn't work those cases alone."

Besides placing Thompson in an unnecessarily risky situation, her sergeant's actions were also contrary to the announced official police policy. In fact, a newspaper article at the time quoted one senior police official as saying, "The addition of female officers to our unit has been most valuable, a real boost to our investigative forces. With the obvious exception of situations where physical strength is involved, we assign our women officers the same cases as we do our men."

"That quote was a lot of bullshit," says Karas. "You seldom had a chance to predict in advance what cases required physical strength or would present the most danger. It wasn't a matter of deciding in each case, well, are you going to have a fight here? Are you going to have a gun battle? You just went out and did your job."

Although the SPD promptly followed the commission's recommendation to disband the Women's Bureau, the department continued to stonewall the women when it came to allowing them to test for promotions alongside the male officers. In 1971, for instance, several policewomen signed up to take the sergeant's exam only to learn that despite earlier promises, the department was not ready to let them test.

"I didn't sign up because I knew it was a loser at that point," Thompson says. "I knew that the department was not going to back us and was in fact going to take the opposite stance. At that time you had to pay one dollar to take the civil service exam. They accepted the dollar from each of the women that signed up, waited until the day of the exam, and then turned the women away at the door."

"We could have sued over their refusal to let us test, and we would have won," Karas notes. "But Frank Moore was the acting chief, and he was a fellow we all respected and liked very much. We didn't want to give him any more trouble because he already had more than he could handle with the department scandals. But if we had been like some women are in the business world we would have sued."

"When the story broke that some of the beat officers were taking payoffs, it was a sticky time," Ejde adds. "A high-profile investigation of the department was conducted, and during that difficult time we had five chiefs in less than five years. One year, we had three. I think the fact that we didn't sue at that time was a pretty fair indication that we cared more about the department as a whole than we did about sitting for promotions."

The women put their push for advancement on hold and, surprisingly, they were rewarded the following year by being allowed to test for sergeant. To this day they don't know whether the decision to let them test was due to internal policies or because of pressure from the outside to promote women. Either way, the exam represented the first time in seventeen years that policewomen were allowed to test for a promotion to sergeant, and the very first time they were competing directly with men.

Three women—Skagen, Thompson and Ejde—scored in the top twenty-five percent and became eligible for promotion.

"They promoted us right in a row," Noreen Skagen recalls. "First Beryl, then Karen, and then myself. And we didn't get it through any affirmative action. They went right down the list and when our names came up, we got promoted. So it wasn't as devastating or as traumatic for the men as it would become. We got some reaction, but it wasn't really hostile. It was more like, 'By God these women know how to take tests, so they're going to be very competitive.' Most of the men took a wait-and-see attitude because we were going into roles that we had never been in before."

As with all new sergeants, the women found themselves transferred to patrol duty to supervise a squad of patrol officers.

Despite the previous experiments in the 1960s with policewomen in patrol, and Thompson's more recent turn in the North Precinct, the department brass remained uncertain about how women would fair out on the street.

"We're experimenting to see if we will run into any obstruction in handling the public and to see what the public's reaction will be," Assistant Chief Richard G. Schoener told a local newspaper at the time. "Obviously, we are not going to assign them to high-density crime areas."

This last point was misleading because the department normally wouldn't assign a new male sergeant to such high-density areas. Even so, Ejde was grateful that her first assignment was a relatively quiet one.

"When I made sergeant," Ejde recalls, "my first assignment was Queen Sector First Watch patrol, which ran from 4 a.m. until noon. It was the largest patrol section in the whole city, but First Watch had the lowest incidents of crime during a shift. I think that was well ordered and probably a good idea, because they had nothing to go on to show how a female patrol sergeant would do. I made a lot of mistakes. Fortunately, none of them were really bad, and nobody got killed."

Despite feeling pressure to succeed, Ejde enjoyed her first assignment and found many of the men to be very supportive.

"During my first roll call as an active duty patrol sergeant, the men presented me with a cigar to carry in my briefcase. I knew the cigar represented a tradition of sorts—it was given to the sergeant to mask the smells of the really bad crime scenes with dead bodies that had been decomposing for days or even weeks. As it turned out, the only time that cigar would have come in handy was when I was called up to an apartment building where a women's body had been on the floor for five or six days. The room was, shall we say, fairly aromatic. That case was upsetting because nobody in the building—not the concierge or the manager—no one had checked up on this woman. Nobody cared enough to realize that she hadn't showed up for meals. After we investigated the scene, my patrol officers said, 'Gosh, you did well. You didn't even have to use your cigar.' "

In addition to the three women appointed sergeant, Mary Stowe, who earned her sergeant's rank in the Women's Bureau back in the mid-fifties, took the lieutenant's exam and became the first woman promoted to that rank. Several years later, Skagen, Thompson, and Ejde followed in her footsteps. When Skagen made lieutenant, she was assigned to the North Precinct where she had worked briefly as a sergeant. While she was familiar to the officers, she still sensed a degree of apprehension.

"When I walked into the room the first day I could tell there was quite a bit of tension," Skagen recalls. "The captain decided to come down in the middle of the night to introduce me and give me a glowing introduction. I was thinking, *Oh, I wish you wouldn't do this. Just let me take this on my own.* When I walked in, he was talking to the officers on my watch and they were all standing at attention. I waited for the captain to finish and leave, and then I said, 'Okay, everybody, sit down.' I started talking to them. I asked them what their concerns were, and they told me. One of their big concerns was that my husband was an assistant chief and that I might go home and tell him if any of them made any mistakes.

"I started to laugh. I replied, 'No. The way our marriage has survived in this job is that we've established protocols. We don't go to lunch together, we don't discuss each other's assignments or anything else. We maintain very separate identities. So you don't have anything to worry about there. What else?' Well, they didn't know if I knew enough about patrol.

"I told them, 'I'm a very fast learner. I don't expect to be out here as an authority figure. The authority part of my job is not what counts. What counts is that I give you the support and the kind of guidance you need from the senior officer to help you do your jobs. I'm expecting you to help me do it. And I've got the door open. If you have any gripes or complaints, or you have any needs or feel frustrated about something, you walk in my door and let me know.' That cut the ice. As far as they were concerned, I was still in a 'show me' situation, but I think our talk made them feel more comfortable."

Although her introduction at roll call seemed to ease some concerns, Skagen still faced the challenge of convincing the sergeants who would serve under her that she was up to the job. To help convince them, she met individually with each of the sergeants and visited all the districts in her precinct.

"I had one sergeant who was so distressed about having a woman commander that he took four vacation days the day I arrived," she notes. "Of course, his squad didn't help him any. They put cartoons on his desk, a big sign on the bulletin board, and they just really made his life miserable. He was absolutely devastated. Four days later he came back with every intention of putting in his request for transfer. But he was a professional—an old-school sergeant—and so he asked me if I wanted to tour his district so he could point out some of the problems. I said, 'Yes, I would really appreciate that.' We went out and he was very pleasant.

"Before we got back to the station, I said, 'I'm well aware of how you feel about a woman commander and I fully understand. If you feel uncomfortable working with me, you've got an excellent record here on the department, you're very well respected, and I will give you whatever you need in the way of a recommendation to get you into another assignment with no hard feelings. But you're the senior sergeant, and if you stay on I could learn from your wisdom and guidance. I would really appreciate it if you would consider staying on.' Then we parted for that day. The next morning he walked in and said he was going to stay.

"When I left that assignment, all the officers lined up to say goodbye, and this particular sergeant came over to me and said,

'I would work for you anywhere. You're the finest lieutenant I have ever worked for. If you ever need me just let me know. And if I can ever get back into whatever unit you are in I am going to do it.' So, whatever it was, my approach to the job worked, and I carry that moment as one of my prizes. As far as I'm concerned it was one of the nicest things that ever happened to me."

One policewoman who did not advance to sergeant or higher was Helen Karas. While Karas took the sergeant's exam in 1972, she scored one point down from the top twenty-five and decided not to test again.

"I never took another exam because I figured I was happy working where I was," she explains. "I was working in the fraudulent checks unit, arresting felons and enjoying it. And, at my age at that time I didn't want to go out on the street in uniform to supervise a patrol squad. There was a lot of pressure pushing women into higher positions, but I didn't feel I had the capabilities that many of my colleagues had. I couldn't match Pat and Noreen and Beryl. I had too much trouble figuring out some of the technical details, like working on budgets and things like that, all the things that go with upper-level management. That didn't appeal to me, nor was I good at it."

Karas subsequently decided to retire in 1976 after serving twenty-five years on the department.

"Physically, I had reached the point where I felt I was a hazard," she explains. "I would have left one year earlier but they convinced me to stay on and put me in personnel. That was a good job and I enjoyed the working environment, but by the time I retired, I was ready to go. I don't regret the twenty-five plus years in police work. I figure they were good to me and, really, I had one hell of a good time."

With the Women's Bureau disbanded and policewomen having earned the ranks of sergeant and lieutenant, it appeared that females were finally being accepted throughout the department. Yet, in the mid-1970s one last bastion of maleness remained, and until that citadel was breeched women would never taste true equality.

5

THE FIRST NINE

In the spring of 1976, nine women walked out onto the streets of Seattle and made history. Like the Right Stuff astronauts who blasted off into the uncertainty of space, these women faced an equally mysterious frontier — the all-male world of police patrol.

Although the twenty-one policewomen of the Women's Bureau had made enormous strides towards equality in assignment and promotions, they were still viewed as "policewomen" from a generation when women and men had different roles in police work. All of that changed when the Seattle Police Department hired its first female patrol officers — known collectively as "The First Nine" — and trained them to stand as equals beside the men.

But as the First Nine soon discovered, being trained to be equals was very different from being *treated* as equals. Right from the start, male instructors in the police academy thought they would fail, and male coworkers did not trust them. Worst of all, the women found themselves constantly hounded by rumors about everything from their abilities on the street to their prowess in the bedroom.

"It's probably true that the men really didn't know what to do with us," offers Joanne Hunt. "Although there were twenty-one policewomen on the department, the majority of patrol officers were unfamiliar with them and weren't sure if they should treat us like little sisters or daughters. All their lives they had been protecting us and now all of a sudden they were supposed to depend on us."

Each of the First Nine—Joanne Hunt, Debbie Allen, Leslie
Baranzini, Vicky Burt, Marsha Camp, Mary Kulgren, Mickey
Lee, Terri MacMillan and Peggy Timm—came to police work
from a different direction. Hunt, for instance, had been a
fisheries graduate student and one of the first female scuba
instructors in the nation before discovering she was more
interested in law enforcement. She first hired on with the
University of Washington campus police before applying to the
SPD.

For Peggy Timm, the inspiration to become a police officer
originally came from her older sister, who had flirted with the
idea several years earlier but did not pursue it because the
Seattle Police Department was not hiring.

"What put me over the edge," Timm recalls, "was when I
worked as a waitress at a twenty-four-hour coffee shop and I
regularly waited on police officers. One night I said to them, 'I
want to be what you are, a police officer,' and they all laughed.
Here I was this petite little 5 foot 3 ½ inch waitress talking to
guys who were 6'2". They couldn't believe it when two years
later I was in the academy. They were even more surprised
when later on I worked at the same precinct with them."

For many of the First Nine, the most enticing aspect about
becoming a police officer was not the opportunity to carry a gun
and a badge. It was the pay.

"I was working as a technical artist at Boeing," recalls Debbie
Allen, "and I found out that a male friend was making more
money than I was, even though we were working in the same job
and I had a higher evaluation rating. Until then, it had never
dawned on me that men would be paid more than women as a
part of the pay scale. When I learned the police department offered
the same pay for men and women, I decided to give it a try."

Getting selected to earn that pay proved difficult. The SPD
had not hired officers of either gender in several years, and when
the department announced it was hiring again more than two

thousand men and women applied. Candidates were asked to complete written exams, physical agility tests, background checks, polygraph tests, medical physicals, and an oral board. During the nine-month-long process the women were asked pointed questions about their sexual orientation, what they would do if they got pregnant, even whether or not they'd ever had an abortion.

Once the hiring was completed, less than seventy were selected to attend the academy. More than ten were women. One was African American, the rest white. The cadets were divided into two six-month-long classes, one that started in October 1975 and a second that began in November. Both classes provided the same curriculum and tests, but the women had very different experiences depending on which class they were in.

Those in the October class enjoyed a sense of teamwork with their classmates and found their instructors supportive. However, such feelings of camaraderie were missing from the November class. Instead, the four women who "survived" the second class—Allen, Camp, Kulgren and Timm—found themselves at odds with their male classmates and with each other amid a sea of rumors and suspicions.

"In the academy, every woman was out for herself," says Timm. "I assumed they'd stand together and support each other, but these women wanted to look good in the men's eyes, and if they had to cut one of the women down to do it, they would. The women in the other class were closer to each other, but the women in my class didn't work together or help each other. It was sad. But maybe that was because it was so competitive."

Looking back, many of the women in the November class blame the male tactical instructor—the "Tac" officer—for setting the tone. He frequently played favorites and put the women down.

"What we experienced may have been similar to hazing in boot camp," Allen observes, "except that the women were prime targets. I think in the military everybody goes through the process of proving they should be there, but I don't think everybody in our class went through it. We heard stories from the first class and it sounded like whatever hazing they went through built camaraderie. But our Tac officer did just the opposite. He built distrust of our fellow classmates."

"The academy sergeants and instructors thought having female patrol officers was a fad that wouldn't last," Camp says, "and they believed they would nip it in the bud right there by showing we couldn't take it. So they were pretty hard on us, both mentally and physically, and they would make us run until one of the women threw up. I didn't throw up, but I was always glad somebody else did because then we got to stop.

"I think they fell back on the idea that 'We've got to make *men* out of them,' " she adds. "I don't know what they were saying to the men, but with us it was like, 'We've got to toughen you up because you don't have enough life experiences, and out there on the street the criminals will just eat you up.' "

Individual men were also singled out if they were perceived to be weak, but the women found themselves targeted for a wide variety of reasons.

"I was the youngest at twenty and, at 5'3½" and 108 pounds, the smallest in the academy," Timm recalls. "They were always trying to get me to gain weight, and they were always unhappy that I was short. Every single solitary morning for six months straight in a row, when we lined up for roll call someone would say to me, 'Timm, get out of that hole.' I suppose it was funny, but at the time I didn't feel that way."

"There was a lot of emphasis on her size," adds the 5'4" Allen. "I'm not big, but it was probably to my advantage that there was somebody littler than me. In the driving training we had Dodge Darts with bucket seats and we sometimes had to do high speed driving while going backwards. Seeing over the back of the seat became important, and they made a big issue about whether Peggy was tall enough to see over the back seats."

While Timm was a target due to her size and age, Camp was singled out for confidently speaking her mind.

"I thought the way to answer questions was to give my opinion back," Camp explains. "I was wrong. The academy was the first time I got introduced to the fact that where men are considered knowledgeable, women are called opinionated. Where men are aggressive, women are bitchy. I had never been in a situation before where I was expected to do exactly what the men were doing, and then was told, 'Okay, you did fine *for a woman.'* "

Camp was particularly targeted in mock arrest scenes where police officers played the part of suspects and the academy cadets were asked to place them under arrest. The person being arrested could go easily or be difficult. For Camp's test, the suspect refused to put his hands up even when she had her gun drawn and in his face.

"They made it impossible for her to succeed," Allen notes. "The male class president would go through a mock scene and when he told the mock suspects what to do, they would do it. But Marsha would give her suspects orders and they wouldn't listen to her, and when she called for backup they wouldn't come. On my mock test, the suspects did as I asked, and I was relieved. I don't think Marsha was doing anything differently than I did, but the instructors turned it into a no-win for her, so it looked like she didn't know what she was doing."

One of the most damaging tactics implemented by the academy was to have students evaluate each other and say who they would or wouldn't want to ride with in a patrol car. Both Camp and Timm were rated low by the rest of their class, prompting the training staff to suggest they seek other employment.

"The Tac officer came to me and said, 'Well, Marsha, you might as well quit now because everybody in the class says the number one person they hate is you,' " Camp recalls. "'Oh, really?'

I said. 'Well, thank you for the information. I'm a lot tougher than that and I'm pretty pigheaded. So, you can fire me, but I'm not going to quit.' "

"They suggested to me that I also should leave," adds Timm. "They called me in and said, 'Well, it doesn't look like you're strong. It doesn't look like you can take people down. It doesn't look like you're physically able to do this job.' I was almost in tears because I really wanted to be a police officer, and I remember I left that day thinking I was going to resign. I went home and talked to my boyfriend, my mom, and my sister, and they all said, 'This has been such torture for you. Why don't you just resign?' "

Timm was prepared to do just that until she received a call from another female cadet, who later quit under similar pressure. "She called me up and said, 'Peggy, why in the world would you resign? You've done nothing wrong.' And suddenly I thought, *She's right*. The next day I crawled into the academy. It was one of the hardest things I've ever done in my life. I walked in and said, 'I don't want to resign. I'll do whatever it takes.' "

Through it all, the women found themselves constantly plagued by rumors. One rumor had a particular female cadet getting special treatment due to a supposed relationship with the Tac officer. Adding credence to this claim was the fact that the two knew each other from before the academy. Another rumor had known a different female cadet sleeping with the physical training instructor. Although both women denied the rumors, the allegations further eroded the women's confidence in each other and their male counterparts.

The female cadets in the November class were also given the sense that, ultimately, out on the streets they would be all alone.

"One of the first things they told us was that the citizens hate you, and that all we could count on was each other," Allen recalls. "I could understand this because we were in the mid-1970s after all of the protests. But then they went on to say that as women, well, our coworkers weren't going to accept us either. They gave us the impression that it would be us against the world."

"They definitely came out and said the men would not stand by us in the field," adds Camp. "I never found that to be true. Once I got out of the academy, the men I worked around had the attitude of 'Well, let's see. If she can do the job, then that's fine.' Maybe they didn't give wholehearted support, but they were willing to give me a chance."

By the time the two academy classes ended, nine women remained to graduate, all of them white. However, before they hit the streets, the First Nine faced yet another obstacle—their uniforms. While policewomen of the past carried guns in their purses and wore skirts, the new female patrol officers required uniforms that were consistent with the men's. Since there were no clothiers in the mid-70s who specialized in police uniforms for females, the SPD had to develop its own.

"We looked like a cross between a meter maid and a flight attendant," Hunt laments.

"The uniforms fit horribly," Allen agrees. "They were not user-friendly. Women's pants at the time had zippers on the side and not on the front, and our pants conformed to this rule. Well, every time we wanted to use the bathroom, we had to take off our gun and utility belt. We had no back pockets to carry our radios like the men did, and we couldn't carry notebooks in the front of our shirts because they thought our shirts should be proportional to women's tailoring styles and the pockets were too small."

"They had us wear these crossover ties that snapped in the front," Camp adds, "and hats that I think they must have gotten from United Airlines. They looked like Navy WAVE hats, and when you put the hat brass on them it crunched them down so it looked like you had sat on them. The hats were just terrible."

Within the first few months out on the street, all of the women went on their own to a local tailor and had men's uniforms cut to fit. Although these were also fraught with problems, like shirt pockets that were too close together, the uniforms were considerably more user-friendly.

The women officially hit the streets in the spring of 1976, and they began four months of field training with officers individually assigned to each of them. Again, while some of the women were paired with field training officers—called FTOs—who were friendly and supportive, others found themselves being trained by men who thought females didn't belong in police work.

"The lieutenant that was in charge of the student officers told me he was going to do anything he could to fire me because he didn't think women should be on the police department," Kulgren recalls. "My first FTO was fine, but then the lieutenant put me with a guy who absolutely hated women. This officer repeatedly told me he thought women were to be fucked and that was it. That's what he said as we were driving around the city and he was training me. He couldn't stand me, and he was very up front about it.

"One day I tried to reason with him, but it did no good. I said, 'Look, we're stuck together, like it or not. Why don't you just back off and let me put my time in, and I'll go on to the next one and we'll just kind of forget about this.' But he wouldn't. I went home after that shift and thought, *What am I doing here? This just isn't worth it.* And then I thought, *It's only for a month. I can put up with anything for a short amount of time.* And I did put up with him, but by the end of the month I was a wreck."

Out on the street, the FTO frequently and intentionally provoked fights with drunks and then left Kulgren to deal with them alone.

"He would start yelling at the street person and say, 'She called you this name.' I'd just be standing there flatfooted in disbelief. It was all I could do to get back into the car to save my ass. This went on for several nights and I just put up with it. This guy was such a jerk."

After about three weeks, Kulgren was granted a transfer and enjoyed a better working relationship with her third and fourth FTOs. While none of the other First Nine had such a bad experience during their field training, many of them sensed that the men weren't sure how to react to them.

"I think they were waiting for us women to fail," Timm offers. "No one said, 'We're waiting for you to fail,' but you just knew it. It was just like how they waited for us to fail in the academy. Out on the street, they wanted to see how you'd react to situations. You know how it is—a woman's never done a job before so they assume you can't do it until you prove otherwise. They assumed somehow we would get into a patrol car and see something and go 'Oh, I can't do this. I've got to resign.' Well, that didn't happen. We got good grades and passed the probationary period."

"The crusty old cops were the easiest to sway and to turn around," Vicky Burt notes. "You could do the simplest thing and they were so amazed that this female could do anything that after that they were behind you one hundred percent. They quickly became my biggest supporters."

Besides being tested on the streets, the women also faced teasing in the precincts, a form of testing that would almost certainly be considered sexual harassment today.

"I had been on not too long," Hunt recalls, "and I walked into the roll call one day and one of the older officers looked at me and he said, 'You know, you're kind of cute. I think you're a spinner.' Fortunately, I knew a spinner was a woman that you can set on top of your lap and spin. I looked at him and said, 'At 145 pounds, I would break your turntable.' He laughed and thought it was funnier than hell, and after that we got along fine."

"I wasn't being sexually harassed, I was being tested," she adds. "They teased the new men hard, too. They were testing us to see how we would react. What kind of person are you? Are you going to burst into tears and run away and tell the captain I said a naughty thing to you? Well, then if you do that, how can I trust you to stand up to abuse out on the street?"

Sometimes the toughest reaction came not from the men, but from their wives.

"When I was assigned out at a precinct as watch commander," Noreen Skagen recalls, "I got calls from wives saying they didn't want their husbands working with women partners. I would tell them, 'You don't have any idea if these women are qualified or not. If they're not, or if there's a serious professional problem, then I will deal with it. But if they're doing a good job, they'll stay right where they are.' I told one woman, 'I appreciate how you feel, but wives are not going to dictate the command actions of this department.' I was as pleasant as I could be. I said, 'I really understand your concerns, but let's give it a chance and see what happens.' "

"For some of the married guys, I think the hardest part for them was with their wives," Baranzini adds. "You'd know because the men would say things like, 'She just doesn't feel that I'm as safe with a female officer as I would be with a male officer. I need to call her at such and such a time.' I would say, 'Should I meet her? Shall we take away this unknown?' I made an effort to meet the wife and let her know, 'Yeah, we're in a car together and we have to be able to trust each other and share with each other, but I don't want to take your husband away from you.' Once I did that, they were fine."

Of course, despite such assurances, relationships did blossom between male and female patrol officers. Within one year, eight of the First Nine were dating male officers, and this sudden reality caused the Seattle Police Department management no end of concerns.

"Having male and female patrol officers dating was truly a big change for the department," Allen recalls. "We must have been on for about a year when it came to the attention of one of the assistant chiefs that male and female patrol officers were living together. He had a meeting with the original nine women and, without any men present, said, 'If I find out that there is a woman officer on this department and a man officer living together without being married, they will both be fired.' We all kind of went 'Whoa,' because some of us were already in violation."

Many of the women simply lied about their addresses to cover the fact they were living with one of the men. Eventually, Allen became the first woman on the department to list her real address as that of the male officer she was living with. She did so after a lieutenant pointed out that it was a violation of the police manual if officers did not provide an accurate address and phone number, while there was nothing in the manual that said officers could not live with whomever they wanted.

"Not long after, that particular assistant chief retired," Allen adds, "and there was a realization in the department that the train was moving forward and it wasn't going to stop. That was just one of the adjustments the department had to make, and lots of relationships and marriages developed out of women coming into patrol."

At the same time that the male officers, their wives, and the department were adjusting to the First Nine being out on the streets, the public at large was intrigued.

"Every night we'd hear some citizen say: 'Oh, a policewoman. I'm so glad we have a policewoman out here,' " Kulgren says. "Or, 'It must be just wonderful to be out here with all these men.' Or, 'Oh, you're just so cute. You just don't look like a police officer.' I loved that one."

"People would drive by while we were giving tickets and yell out, 'Hey, get a haircut,' " Teri MacMillan adds.

"I remember getting the fun comments," Allen recalls, "but a lot of times you just got stared at. You felt like you always had to sit somewhere where people couldn't watch you eat because they were just aghast that there was this female in uniform, and heaven forbid they should watch you drool or something. And then there were the kids. I went to an event at Meeker Elementary School for a field day. I was interviewed by kids for the school newspaper and one of the questions was, 'Well, now, does your partner allow you to drive the car sometimes?' This was a natural perception by kids. 'Well, my dad lets my mom drive.' We were just such an oddity at the time. It was kind of fun in some ways, but I don't think anybody is comfortable being under the microscope all the time."

The longer the women worked on the street, the more it became apparent that some citizens still preferred talking to male officers.

"One day I was out with a male partner," Camp recalls. "I was driving, and a person approached our car. First he came up to the driver's side, but when he saw me, he walked all the way around the car and talked to my male partner.

"Later I said to my partner, 'I wonder why he did that?' My partner said, 'Don't you know? It's because you're a woman and you don't know anything.' When he said that he wasn't kidding. He added, 'Haven't you noticed that people have been doing that?' I hadn't, but then I started paying attention and I would notice that people would often come up and talk to him. I got along great with this partner, and I appreciated how he handled this situation. Whenever they would come up to him, he would say, 'I don't know, talk to my partner,' and refer them to me."

If the public at large was surprised, the male criminals were often flabbergasted.

"They were so stunned about seeing a female officer that it kind of took the wind out of their sails," Kulgren recalls. "We would arrest and book them and they would be just absolutely stunned. 'She *arrested* me.' Some of them would just laugh and say, 'I've been arrested by a woman.' And they'd tell everybody in jail about it."

"Very quickly I learned people react more to your voice and the uniform than they do your appearance," Camp offers. "I was amazed at what I could get away with. I was pursuing a guy who had just snatched a purse downtown. He must have been 6'5" tall, but I ordered him to stop and he did. I then turned him around and cuffed him. All he had to do was run and I probably wouldn't have been able to stop him. Being one of the first women was lucky because people weren't used to seeing us. They were stunned for a moment, and that was almost as good as pulling your gun.

"There are times when the only thing you can do is fight," she adds. "That's why the men thought women wouldn't be able to do the job. But when we got out on the streets we realized there was another way to do this. You can say, 'You know, you're going to jail. We can either do it the easy way or I'm going to get my face broken and you'll go anyway.' Some would say, 'Well, I don't care,'" and I'd say, 'Okay, well take your best shot.' Usually they would come around because how macho is it to beat up a 5'3 ¾" woman?"

Ultimately, many of the women found that the hardest part of the job was the constant stream of rumors that seemed to swirl around them.

"There were only nine of us and twelve hundred of them, so rumors were flying," Allen recalls. "All I know is that if I had had sex with every man that the rumors said I had, it would have been a physical miracle."

"I heard more rumors about how we were all sleeping with every officer there ever was," Baranzini adds. "I thought, *Geez, how do we have enough hours in the day to do all of this?* It bothered me that they were talking about us, but what could you do?"

Baranzini proved to be one of the biggest victims of the rumor mill when, after one year on the department, she suddenly learned she was pregnant. The male officers were less than kind. Among other actions, they started up a betting pool on who the father was.

"When I got pregnant it was a shock," she recalls. "I was the first female officer to get pregnant, and I also was not married. Well, it was okay for the guys to mess around and for the married guys to have affairs, but not for me. It would also have been 'okay' to have an abortion and to continue working. But I said 'No. I'm not having an abortion, *and* I want to keep working.' Also, the father wasn't a police officer, so he wasn't somebody in the family. I think that irritated the guys more than anything else."

Besides the personal rumors about individual officers, the women also faced collective rumors that repeatedly suggested they couldn't handle the job.

"The men would tag people with things that they couldn't live down," Kulgren notes. "No matter how many times a woman would deny something, nobody believed her. Whatever the problem, women were the scapegoat."

"When you'd hear a story about somebody really screwing up you'd go, 'Please, God, don't let it be a woman,' " Hunt adds. "I remember we'd been on quite a while when there was a rumor, 'Jesus, some dumbshit detective went in to talk to a suspect and the suspect took his gun.' I remember thinking, *Oh please, let it be a man*. And it was.

"That feeling is something you can't get away from," she adds, "because as a woman if you screw up it reflects on all the women, but if a white male screws up it's just him. I guess there won't be real equality until a woman can do a dumbshit stupid thing and it just becomes 'Officer X did a truly dumbshit thing,' and they don't go, 'See, I told you women couldn't do this job.' "

More than thirty years after the First Nine hit the streets, women are still striving for that equality. But progress has been made, and today more than 180 female officers — white, black, Asian and Latina — work for the SPD in positions throughout the department.

And what of the First Nine? Burt and Baranzini left police work early on to start families, while Kulgren and Lee became detectives, Camp earned the rank of sergeant, and Hunt and Timm became lieutenants. Allen rose to the rank of assistant chief before retiring in 2002. MacMillan, the last to remain on the department, retired in 2007 as a sergeant.

"When I came out of the academy," Debbie Allen reflects, "I thought that I might not stick around because the academy experience had prepared me to expect things to be pretty dismal with my peers. But once I got out on the street I really liked the guys I worked with, and I worked in some great squads where I felt a lot of support. Certainly, there were men who weren't supportive and there were certain men who would never accept that women should be police officers, but, fortunately, they were the minority."

6

THE NEXT WAVE

Although the arrival of the First Nine on the streets proved to be dramatic, the attitudes of regular citizens, the department brass and the male officers were not transformed overnight. With initially only nine female patrol officers among twelve hundred, change came gradually and only as more women were added to the force. Many of these rookie officers found themselves in groundbreaking positions as the first female on their squad or shift, or even at their particular precinct. And, just like the First Nine, each new woman faced unique challenges.

BEING THE FIRST

In May of 1977, eight more women graduated from the academy and hit the streets. Among the rookies were Toni Malliet and Cindy Caldwell, two very different women whose careers would have a lot in common. On the surface, their differences were skin deep — Malliet is African American, while Caldwell is white with blond hair and blue eyes. Yet both women rose up through the ranks to achieve the status of Captain and Assistant Chief respectively. They found themselves followed by controversy and rumors throughout their careers, and ultimately proved to be survivors.

"One of my earliest assignments was in the East Precinct," recalls Malliet, who hired on under her maiden name of Harrell. "Well, I was born and raised in that neighborhood, so I was home. I couldn't go ten minutes down the street without being recognized as Florence's daughter, Idel's granddaughter,

Keith's sister. My brother and my cousins were excellent ballplayers and well known, and everyone knew the Harrell name."

Malliet was unique because she was the first African American female patrol officer, and only the second black woman to serve on the SPD. She followed in the footsteps of policewoman Lillian Mitchell, who worked on the Women's Bureau in the late 1950s and early '60s.

"Being an African American woman in a police uniform made me a real novelty," Malliet explains. "My partner and I would go into the black community to a disturbance where everybody was yelling and screaming, and the next thing I knew, everyone had stopped to look at me. Someone would say, 'You're a woman.' *Yeah, so?* I had people apologize to me for swearing in front of me. I loved it, and I quickly learned how to use this to my advantage. If someone started using colorful language, I would turn to them and politely say, 'I certainly would appreciate it if you wouldn't swear in front of me.' And they would apologize! It was a great way to calm people down so we could talk. My male partners were going, 'Huh?' because this never happened to them.

"Early on in my career, a fellow officer told me that at the end of each day the only thing I was supposed to do was to come back in the same condition as when I left," she adds. "I took that literally and had a lot of fun with that. If somebody on the street wanted to fight me, I would show them my fingernails and say, 'Do you see these fingernails? You know, it really would upset me if I break one of these nails. You're going to jail either way, but I will really be upset if I break one of these nails.' They would think I was crazy, but it worked."

Besides being the first black female officer on the department, Malliet often found herself in the position of being the first female of any kind wherever she was assigned.

"I was the first woman to work the South Precinct," she notes, "and we had standup roll call where we were expected to appear on time. If you looked at the clock and realized you were running late, you would run out of the locker room and tell the sergeant you were there. Well, a couple of times the sergeant would say, 'Stand up!' and guys who were late would run out of the locker room in their underwear. Then they'd see me and go, 'Oh, yeah, I forgot there was a woman here.' They didn't do it to embarrass me, so I didn't mind. I just thought it was funny.

"Probably about three months later, they did send another woman down. Since there was no shower for women, when we wanted to shower we would invade the men's locker room, knock and yell, put a sign up on the door, and go in and take showers. No one played pranks on us. I never had my car sabotaged. Never had nasty notes put on my locker. They may have disliked me and hated me and talked about me like a dog, but they never did it to my face. And they never hindered me from doing my job."

Malliet's early career was fraught with controversy. A few years after she hired on, a scandal swept the South Precinct where she was assigned. Many male officers were investigated and subsequently fired for illegal drug activity. Malliet was incriminated as well, and she too was fired. Later, after a civil service hearing, she was exonerated and hired back. Despite being cleared of all charges, Malliet found that the stigma of her arrest continued to follow her throughout her years on the department.

"You can't understand how much it haunts me everyday," she says. "I was in limbo for six months fighting the department, and I prevailed. But when everything is rescinded, you don't get the big newspaper article. You get a tiny little blurb saying, 'This officer is exonerated of all charges and reinstated.' I'm still suffering from it twenty years later. The nicknames—'Snow Queen'—and the rumors continue even today. It doesn't change. That was a horrible experience."

Other controversies plagued her throughout her years on the department, including unsubstantiated claims that she interfered with investigations when she was a precinct commander. Malliet says she doesn't know whether all the rumors were due to her being African American, because she is a woman, or because she is Toni.

"Maybe it's a combination of all three," she wonders. "I don't want to say it's because I'm black or because I'm a woman. I always say it's because of who I am, and that's just Toni. I can't control the other things, but I can control who I am and how I act."

Although not as dramatic, Cindy Caldwell's career also involved numerous challenges. Tall and blonde, Caldwell has a tendency to be blunt and say what she thinks, and this personality trait sometimes landed her in hot water. Her challenges began in the academy when she started dating one of the male cadets, prompting the staff to take unusual action.

"One day, they pulled all the women out of our academy class," Caldwell recalls, "and two female officers came in and told us, 'Do not date cops because they all talk about you, and if you're seen with one, it will be all over the place.' Well, that was funny because they both were dating cops. Then I thought, *Why didn't they call all the men in and tell them not to date women on the department?* They were all dating their secretaries. It was totally wrong for them to have brought us in. It was really awkward because there were two assistant chiefs who were married to each other at the time. What standard were they setting? I told them that it was none of their business, and basically said, 'I'm doing great in the academy and you can't touch me.' They knew as a female I could cause some problems, so they called in my boyfriend at the time and yelled at him."

Despite the dating lectures, Caldwell found the academy to be reasonably supportive. Once she hit the streets, however, she felt isolated and alone.

"Okay, so I graduate from the academy really high in my class, and I'm thinking I'm hot shit," she recalls. "I get out onto the street and I'm the only woman on the entire watch. Two of the precincts would not allow 'those cunts' into their precincts, and there were no female supervisors in my precinct all the way up the chain of command. I don't think there was a female supervisor in patrol at the time. They just threw us to the wolves. I empathize with that one female at the Citadel Military Academy because we were thrown out with no support. Most of the guys just ignored me, some of them were real nice and some were vicious. I noticed the worst performing people were the ones who were the most vicious. They didn't have good self esteem in themselves so they lashed out."

"Lashing out" came in many different forms, from verbal harassment to various radio-related games like cutting Caldwell and the other women off when they were reporting calls, or laughing at them over the radio.

"I worked with a couple of guys who were just ridiculous—you know, macho," Caldwell explains. "They would always tell the latest women stories, and say to me, 'You women don't belong here. I wouldn't let my wife do this job.' Or I'd hear comments like, 'We used to have to find our own chickies—girlfriends behind the wives' backs—but now they issue them to us.' Or, 'Now I've got my own secretary.' And they'd talk about our sex lives. When I first came on, they had a list on the wall of who'd done who, and a contest going on to predict who would sleep with which female next. They knew our names, they knew where we lived, they knew what we dressed like, they knew everything about us. That's all they talked about. It was constant. Not by everybody, but by about ten percent, and those are the guys who could make you miserable."

However, Caldwell quickly realized that the men did not hold all of the cards, and that she in fact had her own recourse.

"You could play the guys," she explains. "A lot of the women became quite good at that, and so did I. You had to win the men over one by one. You had to be extra nice and extra helpful, and ignore all the crap that they did. You had to do different things with different men because some needed you to be like their mother. So you'd go, 'Okay, tell me all about your problems.' Some men wanted you to be more flirty. Fortunately, some men just wanted you to do your job and be professional, and with them you didn't have to play a game to fit in. But no matter what, you had to make sure you got into a fight and didn't run away from hard work. You had to do the best on the tests, be the best in sports, and be the best in everything so the men couldn't say anything bad about you.

"Every time I went to a new precinct or got transferred to a different shift or squad, I had to prove myself all over again. I remember the first day I got transferred to the burglary unit, they were expecting a new secretary and the detectives thought I was the secretary. The sergeant cleared his throat and said, 'No, she's the new detective.' One male detective responded: 'Oh, shit. Thank God I'm retiring in fifty days.' "

Caldwell and other women experienced additional stress and anxiety due to the constant on-the-job tension with her male counterparts.

"Our job pays well, it is interesting, and it has a certain status in the outside world," she observes. "It is very secure, and I don't think I could work anywhere else. But the downside is that male officers have a high suicide and divorce rate, and high stress and high substance abuse. Well, whatever the guys have, the women have it worse, with higher levels of everything—from grinding your teeth to ulcers. As a patrol officer I used to come to work and I never once worried about getting hurt. Instead, I was always worried about who was going to insult me today, who was going to put a condom in my car today, or who was going to call out a raspberry as I was walking down the street. We women had all that stress to deal with in addition to the normal concerns of getting into a fight with a drunk or getting shot."

More "firsts" occurred when a new batch of women arrived at the end of the 1970s. Among them was Rosa Melendez, the first Latina on the Seattle Police Department, who arrived at the SPD after having worked for the police department in Salt Lake City. In Utah, she encountered more prejudice for her Hispanic heritage than her gender; in Seattle, her sex was the sole issue.

"In the Seattle academy I found the mock situations were made more difficult for the women than the men," explains Melendez, who achieved the rank of lieutenant before being appointed the first Latina U.S. Marshal by President Bill Clinton in 1994. "I'll tell you one incident that I use in a lot of speeches. It was physical training class and I was supposed to be the police officer who was going to arrest somebody on the street. We were doing this scenario and I got punched in the face twice. I didn't think anything of it until lunchtime when the classmate who punched me said, 'Rosa I'm really, really sorry. I didn't mean to do it but I was ordered by the physical training instructor to punch you in the face as much as I could to see how you would take it.' I said, 'Well, thank you for telling me but I can't believe you would be so stupid that you'd follow that order.' It was not a requirement for any of my other male classmates to get punched in the face.

"I give speeches to young people, women groups, even men's groups. When I do I say, 'I want you to understand now that I am one of the highest ranking women of color in the United States, because nobody outranks a U.S. Marshal. But that sergeant is still a sergeant, and that officer is still an officer.' That makes me feel good now, of course, but back then I got angry. Interestingly, by trying to make things harder on me, and I say it in Spanish, they gave me *guanos*—they gave me guts. 'You won't make me flunk. You have just made me stronger.' "

Out on the street, Melendez discovered the double standard continued.

"East Precinct had more females than the South Precinct and in some ways had more stories about how bad they were," she says. "A lot of the stories were myths. You always heard the story about how the female officer discharged her gun accidentally. I remember one time when I was in internal affairs as a sergeant. It was time for our unit to qualify on our firearms, and our captain was handling one of his weapons in the office. He thought he was dry firing—practicing—and he thought his gun was unloaded. It wasn't. He fired off a round in his office and the bullet went into the wall. That happens all the time during qualifications, more than the public knows. Well, everybody came running into *my* office. I remember saying, 'You guys, look how sexist you are. Every time there's a gun that fires, you assume it's me.' We had a laugh about that, but it *was* sexist. Never once did they ever think it could be one of their fellow men. They automatically went to the only female on the floor to see if she had fired her gun."

Another new hire in 1979 was Carol Minakami, who arrived on the scene with unique physical training skills that made her instantly famous in the department.

"I had been a karate instructor, had competed internationally, and was a third-degree black belt," Minakami explains. "As a result, I came on with a much bigger reputation than I really deserved. I was the first woman to work patrol in the South Precinct Rainier Valley at nights, and before I got there I heard that South was supposed to be no-woman's land where no female would ever be able to make it. They called it 'Siberia,' and the male officers were all supposed to be drunks who hated women and were half crazy. But when I got there I discovered the guys were great. I think a lot of it had to do with my martial arts training. I came in with the reputation that 'Oh, man, she can kick your ass.' Of course, that was exaggerated, but it worked."

While her reputation as a black belt proved helpful when her police career began, Minakami later found that it made little difference to certain men who questioned her abilities for no other reason than she was a woman.

"I've been on the department for more than twenty years," she says, "and I've experienced prejudice two times in my career. First, when I taught at the academy I worked for a sergeant who just hated women. Before I had even arrived he told people that he didn't think women should teach physical training and defense tactics. He thought it was an embarrassment, and he said he was going to get rid of me. He made my life miserable and, eventually, I did switch assignments.

"The second time was when I became the first woman ever to be on the SWAT team. I was there for four-and-a-half years, first as an officer and then as a sergeant. My people treated me very well, but it was hard dealing with officers from other agencies. We went to a lot of joint trainings, and during the Goodwill Games we trained with other SWAT teams from around the state. At one of the trainings I remember walking into this room of fifty to sixty men, and I could feel them looking at me with a feeling like, 'Who brought the woman?' Being on the SWAT team was stressful because you knew the men were watching you, and you got the feeling, 'God, I'd better not screw up.' But once the guys saw that I was trying to do the best I could do and that I wanted to compete fairly, they accepted me.

"Throughout my whole career there hasn't been a lot of noise," concludes Minakami, who earned the rank of sergeant. "Do you know that Life cereal commercial, 'Let Mikey eat it'? Well, my whole career has basically been, 'If we have to have a woman in there, get Minakami.' I think that was the feeling when there was a big push to get a woman on the SWAT team.

Everybody was running scared with affirmative action to get women to fill certain quotas, and basically the feeling was, 'Oh, God. If we have to get a woman, it might as well be her.' "

New "firsts" continue up to the present day.

"I am the first East Indian officer on the department," says Officer Daljit "Dolly" Gill, who joined the Seattle Police Department in 2008 at the age of twenty-seven. "I was born and raised in Seattle, but my parents are from India. They are both practicing Sikhs, but I am not. I go to church, but I am too Americanized to live that lifestyle, and it would be very difficult to do so and be a police officer."

For Gill, the biggest challenge about being a police officer does not come from her coworkers, or from the public—it comes from her East Indian family and friends who don't understand why as a woman she wants to be involved in crime fighting.

"My parents were upset at first because I was working in the medical field and they wanted me to stay in that profession," she explains. "They thought it was more appropriate for a female and they were worried that I wasn't big enough or strong enough to be a police officer."

Gill's parents became more supportive once they realized how much she wanted to be a police officer, but other members of her family were not so open-minded.

"A lot of my relatives ask me, 'Why are you a police officer?' It's like they're saying, 'You're a girl, you're not supposed to do that kind of work.' In a very traditional household, the primary role of the Indian female is to be a housewife, to cook and clean, to take care of the in-laws, her husband, her children. Then, after that, if she has time she can work.

"Being twenty-seven and single is also not good. Every time I speak to my grandmother or other relatives, they say, 'Why aren't you married? It's not good that you're not married.' It's not that they don't respect me. It's just how they were raised. They're having their culture shock now. It's more important to them that I get married than it is for them to know I'm happy in a job."

"It makes me feel that I need to be more in touch with my cultural background," she adds. "Besides being a police officer, I am dating a white guy and I'm perceived by some as going against my culture. With the Indian culture, a lot of people judge you based on whether you are a good Indian female — someone who does what her parents want and who goes with our culture. In the back of my head, that's pressure. Yes, I am the first Indian on the department, and I know the SPD is happy to have me because I am a good person and I add to diversity. But I want to be known as that good Indian cop, not as someone who has upset her parents, went against her culture and became a cop."

Gill admits with a laugh that sometimes she feels trapped in an impossible conflict.

"I try not to dwell on what people think anymore. I used to as a kid, but as an adult I understand people are going to believe what they want and you can't always change their opinions. Sometimes I avoid family functions because I don't want to be interrogated on why I'm not listening to my parents, or why I am upsetting my parents.

"At the same time I think a lot of the Indian population think it's cool that there is an Indian on the department. I can speak both Hindi and Punjabi languages, and they feel represented. I've had to translate a couple of times now. On an armed robbery call at a 7-11 store, officers needed to get a suspect description from the clerk. The clerk didn't speak English and he was wearing a turban, so an officer who remembered me suggested I might be able to help. I think the clerk felt really comforted by the fact that I could interpret for him.

"The East Indian community in Seattle is not very large, and every Indian knows everybody else," Gill adds with a smile. "After I finished interpreting the clerk asked me who my parents were and what town in India they were from. There is only one Sikh church in Seattle, and it turned out he had a friend who knew my parents. Everybody at church knows I am a police officer, and I'm sure they heard about how I interpreted for the shop clerk. I'm sure they also know I'm dating a white guy, and other details of my life. I've learned to accept this because my business has become public."

FAMILY MATTERS

Many of the new female officers came to the SPD with children and families at home. For some, explaining why they wanted to be police officers was difficult when their parents were involved. For others, like Detective Linda Patrick, learning how to explain her job to her children was even more problematic.

"I was attending the University of Washington while going through a divorce, driving a bus, and bussing tables," she recalls. "I saw a poster that said the Seattle Police Department was encouraging minorities to apply. I had never thought about police work before, but when I saw the poster it stopped me in my tracks. I looked at the qualifications—no felony convictions, valid Washington State driver's license, a high school diploma or a GED. Then I saw the salary and I thought, *That's more than I'll get when I finish at the university. Why am I going to school?* Then I thought, *What does police work involve?* Well, I told myself, you get paid to drive around in a car. I love driving fast. And I'm really intrigued by people and their behavior—why they do what they do and what motivates them. I thought, *Man, I could do that all day as a police officer.* So I wrote down the telephone number and applied. I took a test in October of 1979, and I was in the academy the following March. When I got the phone call telling me to report to the academy, I was shocked. What had I gotten myself into?"

Patrick was not the only one who wondered what she was doing. Her two daughters were ages eight and nine at the time, and they did not like the idea of their mother becoming a cop.

"They thought the job was what they saw on TV, and they were frightened. They said, 'Oh, you're going to get killed. That's not a good thing to do, and we don't want you to do it.' I told them it wasn't like TV, and they just had to trust that I knew what I was doing. They got used to my job, but I had to make adjustments. For instance, I had them change their school. First, I didn't want to work around schools where they might be attending because I grew up with my step dad as a principal of a high school, and that always caused a bit of a burden for me. Second, I didn't want them to have a fellow student come up to them and say, 'Okay, your mom's a cop and she just arrested my dad.' So I had them transfer to schools outside of Seattle.

"My daughters eventually adjusted to my being a police officer," Patrick adds, "but I also realized I couldn't tell them what I was really doing. When I was first on the department I was working nights, and I would come home in the morning to have breakfast with them and see them off to school. In the beginning, I would come home excited by what had happened during my shift, and I'd tell them how I'd chased some guy down the street, traveling at one hundred miles per hour, and how my car crashed and all this stuff went flying. Well, my kids would sit there at the breakfast table in shock. They didn't want to hear it because it was too scary. Every time I told them about the details of my day, they'd say, 'We don't want you to go back to work.' So I just quit telling them about the exciting parts. After that, when they asked how my day was I'd just say, 'Work was okay,' and leave it at that.' "

IF YOU CAN'T BEAT THEM, ACT LIKE THEM

As many of the female officers have explained, the day-to-day realities of working in a male-dominated profession created enormous pressure to perform and to fit in. Some coped with the stress by keeping their heads down and doing their jobs. But a noticeable number of new recruits started acting in a way the policewomen of an earlier era never did: they became more and more like the men.

"I heard that some of them were trying too hard to be like the boys, and I could see it too," recalls policewoman Helen Karas. "The way the women swaggered, the way they talked. I don't know if they were really conscious of it at the time, but I think they wanted so much to fit in and be accepted that they started acting like the men."

"I think I tried to be just like one of the guys," admits Sergeant Marsha Camp. "I didn't smoke cigars, but I did drink and swear a bit. It was hard for me to assimilate, and I went through a period where I acted a lot like the men. Women today come on the department saying, 'I don't have to put up with that. You can't make me be just like the men.' And I think, *Yeah, they're right*. But it was a difficult idea to get used to because after twenty years of being brainwashed that you have to do things the way the male officers do, it was hard to think differently."

"I know we got accused of walking like men," Vicky Burt adds. "But I think one reason was that in order to get our arms around our gun belts and everything we've got on them, we had to hold our arms out a little bit, and we got accused of not walking like women anymore. Also, as officers you learn to go into a situation and take immediate control by your tone of voice, your body language, and your mannerisms. I think that could be perceived as us 'acting like a male,' but it was more a way to do the job, and it flowed out into every aspect of your life, whether you were going to school to talk about your kid's progress report or going to a meeting."

"I had a partner name Mickey and she was an outstanding woman," Captain Malliet recalls. "We were the first female partners. Two days a week we worked down King sector, and two days a week we worked David sector, and then we worked by ourselves when we worked Magnolia. They called us the PPP—the Powder Puff Patrol—and it was great. But Mickey was one of the First Nine in patrol, and when she used to come to work she had something to prove. She was going to be just like the fellows. She was a beautiful gal, but she wore her hair in a bun, wore combat boots, had the gloves, and would not wait for backups. At the end of the shift when she walked out of here, everything went into the locker, her hair came down, makeup went on, and that was it. But on duty she told me she had to be just like them. I never felt I had to prove I could be a police officer. But there were a few out there who felt they did, and she was one of them."

"When the women first came on, I worried about that," notes Noreen Skagen, who rose from policewoman to the rank of Assistant Chief. Skagen retired from the Seattle Police Department in 1988 after President Ronald Reagan appointed her to be the first female U.S. Marshal for the Western District of Washington. "I don't think you have to walk like a man and talk like a man and use the language of a man in order to be accepted by them. I haven't seen it work necessarily, and I've heard a lot of ridicule as a response to that kind of style. I've hired a lot of women as marshals and as police officers and I tell them, 'You don't have to do that, you can be yourself. You don't have to change your values in order to belong here. Learn your job, do it the best you can, support the people who work with you, and you will get along fine.' "

One woman who watched the new female patrol officers from a unique vantage point on the street was former policewoman Marlynn McLaughlin. Although McLaughlin initially became a detective when the Women's Bureau disbanded, she later became the only policewoman to transfer to patrol to become a permanent full-time beat cop. She remained in that position until she retired in 1998.

"I've never been one of the boys, and never wanted to be," Officer McLaughlin says. "The women who act like men do so because they want to be accepted. Apparently they don't quite have enough confidence, or they're new and they don't want to go against the grain. That's just the sign of inexperience. As you get older and a little time under your belt you can be more feisty like I am. When I was new on the department I also didn't say too much. You need to learn how the game is being played and test the waters. You don't want to walk in like you own the whole world because you don't want to piss off the wrong people, not if you like your job. But I never felt I had to act like a man to fit in.

"When I worked traffic, an officer safety issue came up," she adds. "It is amazing how people don't see you when you're standing in the middle of the street directing traffic. Working baseball games or other events, for instance, there were numerous times when people would drive right up to my kneecaps before they'd stop. The worst events were the monster truck rallies with all the rednecks in their four-wheel-drives who had been doing a little drinking or a little smoking. Being visible became a concern, so I went out and got a short raincoat that wasn't really authorized and got some reflective patches put on it to make myself more noticeable. We also had these little glow-in-the-dark gloves we could wear, but people wouldn't pay attention to those so I had my nails done with bright neon orange polish. And it worked. From then on, when I'd be out directing traffic, nobody hit me, and people would come up from a block away and say, 'We saw your nails. They look pretty cool.' The guys in my squad would say, 'Watch out, Marlynn really gets in a bad mood if she breaks a nail.' And after every arrest, they'd ask, 'Break any nails Marlynn?' "

A QUESTION OF COURAGE

One of the key issues all new officers must face is whether or not they will stand their ground when the going gets tough. For the women, the question of courage hung on everybody's mind, and it proved to be a lightning rod for rumors.

"A male officer's biggest fear," Detective Linda Patrick explains, "is that when he's in a big fight, the first person to arrive is going to be a female and she's not going to be able to do what a male could do physically. So as a new officer you had to prove you would stand your ground to get rid of their doubts. The other thing you had to do was at some point you had to kick somebody's butt. I hate to use that phrase, but to get accepted you had to kick somebody's butt so that the male officers knew you could do that."

"I recall one time when a local TV reporter did a story because some male officers said there were female officers who couldn't be counted on for backup," says Assistant Chief Debbie Allen. "Those kinds of rumors were frustrating because there was no way to know if they were true or not. Fortunately for me, I was never the subject of any of those rumors, but other women were. There were a lot of rumors going around in those days. Some of the male officers—and it is important to emphasize that it was only *some* of them—were less supportive of having women or any kind of diversity on the department. Unfortunately, they used this reporter as a forum to make their complaints known. It was very frustrating."

"When I first came on," Assistant Chief Cindy Caldwell recalls, "I would lay awake at nights thinking, *What if I can't do this.*" I did okay in the academy, but I kept wondering, what if I go out on the street and I really can't do it? Like a fight breaks out—what if I can't fight with the guy? As it turned out, I was in a few fights and I did fine. But those concerns haunted me when I was a rookie.

"On one of my very first calls, this suspect was running away just as three or four patrol cars were arriving at the scene," she adds. "We all got out and started chasing him, and I just happened to be closer so I caught up to him quicker than anyone else. I didn't know exactly what I was going to do with him because I hadn't been in a real fight on the street yet, but as I reached for him he was so drunk that he tripped and fell flat on his face. I was so close behind him that I landed right on top of him, and I quickly put handcuffs on him. I looked around and the other officers were going, 'Oh, wow!' They were very impressed. Well, that story went all around the squad and made me very popular, and all the time I kept thinking, *Hey, I didn't do anything.* But they didn't know that and I sure wasn't going to tell them."

"Some of the better male officers will admit that there are cowards in both genders," notes Sergeant Lis Eddy. "That's really what it comes down to. Are you a coward? I've heard some male officers say, 'There are some women officers I'd rather have back me than so-and-so.' And he might be a huge guy. Some guys get a reputation for being cowards because they never arrive on a call first, and they only show up when the coast is clear. There are some women who also have that reputation. What people are really looking for is, are you willing to get in there and mix it up?"

"When I came out of the academy," Captain Wanda Barkley recalls, "the first tussle I got into involved a drunk downtown. My FTO and I had the guy up against a wall and the guy started lifting off the wall. My FTO grabbed onto him and took him to the ground and they were wrestling around. I was just standing around watching, and my FTO yelled, 'Grab an arm!' I immediately grabbed an arm, and we quickly got the suspect locked up. Later, my FTO asked, 'Why didn't you do something?' I replied, 'Well, I was waiting for you to do the jujitsu step and throw him over your shoulder, and I didn't want to get in the way and throw you off balance. I was waiting for you to do what on TV you would normally have done.'

"He said, 'This is not TV. Just grab an arm and do whatever you can.' From then on I understood. But I was fortunate that the

FTO was willing to ask that question because someone else might not have. We faced a lot of questions as women about whether we would be there when things got bad. He could have not asked and instead started a rumor. It would have gone around the department, 'Wanda didn't do anything.' Rumors like that did circulate. Fortunately, he did ask me and, from his mindset, the minute he said, 'Do something,' I did everything I was supposed to do."

"I think the backup issue diminished quickly," Captain Malliet says. "I had a partner who was initially afraid I wouldn't be there for him. He used to bring in handgrips for me to use in the patrol car to strengthen me up. One day we got into a fight with a suspect. After we subdued the guy, my partner told me, 'You know, my biggest fear was that if I got into a fisticuff you wouldn't be there for me. But you were there. That's all I want from a partner, to be in there one hundred percent like I am, whatever your one-hundred-percent capacity is.'

"My very first assignment out of the academy was walking a beat downtown," she adds. "Downtown First Avenue twenty years ago was a lot different than it is now. Back then it was lined with hardcore bars, triple-X-rated movie theaters, peep shows, and a lot of hardcore alcoholics. At that time, male officers on the beat had the mentality that if anyone looked at you wrong or talked to you wrong, they went to jail. It was a real 'my way or no way' mentality.

"My first FTO would go looking for fights. There were some people out on the street who would wake up drunk and start trouble. Well, my FTO would remember those folks, and he would go find them and wake them up. I remember telling him one day that I was going to go the whole week without fighting one person. I told him I would still take everybody to jail who needed to go, but I would do so without having to fight one person. He said, 'OK, go ahead,' and I did. Without putting anybody at risk, I just took a few extra minutes to talk the people I was arresting into getting into my car. And they did, without my ever having to put my hands on them. Later my FTO evaluated me down for it because I was talking people into going to jail, but I went the whole week without getting into a fight. And I don't think I've been in two fights since then. I worked the streets for seven years as a patrol officer and three-and-a-half as a lieutenant, and I don't think I had to put my hands on anyone after that.

"Men are doing the same thing today," Malliet concludes. "The mentality has changed — policing has changed — and I think it has a lot to do with women. Women don't have the brute strength and I openly admit that. When I'm with my partner who is 6'2" and 220 pounds, and we go up to somebody and he says, 'Come here,' they comply. But I'm 5'7" and 130 pounds. If I'm by myself, I'm going to smile at you and show you how much charm I have, talk to you real nice, and we're going to jail anyway. You use the tools that you have. It's called smart. I think women have changed our approach and our way of thinking. And society has changed along with it."

"I remember this one guy I pulled over for reckless driving — speeding, swerving, and running red lights," says Detective Patrick. "I pulled him over and right from the start he said I was a racist, and he called me all sorts of names. He had his radio turned up and when I asked him for his license and information, he said, 'I can't hear you.' Finally, I got to the point where I'd had it, and I told him to step out of his car. He said, 'I'll get out of the car. In fact, I'm going to kick your ass.' He came at me, took his belt off, and acted like he was going to hit me with his belt. I radioed for backup but, at that point, he and I were in the middle of the roadway and he started coming towards me. I backed up, and I thought, *I need to do something here because I'm all by myself*. So I told him, 'Well, I'm not going to fight you in the street here. Cars are going by and we're going to get hit or run over.' He stopped for a moment, looked around and said, 'Oh, yeah.'

"This is when I learned that people will do what you tell them to," she adds with a laugh. "I told him, 'Step up on the curb and then we'll fight.' He turned sideways to do so, and I thought, What an idiot. As soon as he turned sideways, I jumped on his back and took him down. I wrestled around with him and kept him up on the curb until my backup got there. While I was waiting, I learned one other thing. I was really short and he was really tall, and I obviously couldn't subdue him by just hitting him. So I realized I just had to hang on to an arm, twist it up behind his back, and do whatever I could to stop him from beating the crap out of me."

When Patrick got the man to the station, he suddenly became very apologetic. Her sergeant reviewed the case and suggested she simply issue the man a citation for reckless driving and release him. She objected.

"I remember saying to my sergeant, 'No, this is a gender thing. He thought that because I was a woman he was going to kick my butt. Well, he's going to jail. I don't care how sorry he is now, he wasn't sorry out there.' Later I found out he was really buff, really strong, and a semi-pro boxer. Fortunately, he was also very drunk. Obviously, if I had tried to fight him it wouldn't have fazed him. What I learned from that was that it doesn't matter how big they are. So the guy's a semi-pro boxer? I still did what I had to do."

Learning how to survive on the streets is crucial for any police officer, but female cops in particular have developed some unusual ways to avoid confrontations whenever possible.

"One thing I always do is keep a roll of Lifesavers in my pocket," explains Officer Mary Ann Parker, who hit the streets in 1986. "When somebody's really going crazy, I pull it out and say, 'Do you want a Lifesaver?' They usually go, 'Yeah,' and they take it and the confrontation is over. Their anger is gone. You learn little tricks. All you have to do is treat people with respect and communicate with them, and most — almost all of them — are very respectful of you."

Although Parker admits there are suspects who can't be tempted by Lifesavers to go peacefully to jail, she's quick to add that most of the fights she has been involved in were actually started by a fellow officer.

"There are times when you do get into tussles with people," she notes, "but I have rarely ever gotten into a fight with a suspect that wasn't first started by another male officer. It begins with this confrontation between these two male egos. It's like two roosters. They start puffing up their feathers. Name calling seems to be real offensive to a lot of men, and that sets them off. I've been called everything, and you just have to let it roll off your back. But guys don't let it roll off. Also, men have more of an approach of 'Do what I say, and that's it. I'm the law.' In one circumstance I had a prisoner in custody in my car under control in handcuffs. I'd arrested him for auto theft. A male officer came over, opened the door and started yelling at him, telling him, 'Don't ever come to my beat again.' The male officer then explained that I was the nice officer, and that if he had made the arrest, the suspect would be going to the hospital now.'

"There have been other situations where I was talking to someone and the male officer didn't like what that person said to me," she adds. "The male officer jumped in and said something like, 'You don't talk to her like that or call her names.' I've actually had to hold the male officer back once and say, 'Now just wait a minute. Let us work this through.' There have been lots of situations where I've been at a scene where an officer is going to make an arrest and the tension just kept building and building because the officer and the suspect were chipping at each other. Suspects love to antagonize male officers, and the male officers — not all of them, but a good portion of them — rise to the bait and the situation becomes physical."

Male officers may be more aggressive on average, but there are also some female officers who are not beyond causing fisticuffs of their own.

"There were times I didn't want a certain male officer to back me up," Marshal Rosa Melendez notes, "and there were times when I didn't want a specific female officer to back me up. There were some guys who, when radio said they were coming to back me up, I thought, 'Oh, hell, I don't feel like fighting today,' because I knew we'd end up in a confrontation with the suspect. There were also some women who felt they had to use their mouth and be real macho who also tended to get into fights. Regardless of their gender, these were officers who didn't know how to interact with people without starting a fight."

While all of the female officers at one time had to face a test of courage out on the street, some proved they had what it takes by surviving a much harsher test—getting injured in the line of duty. Some of the wounds proved to be relatively minor, while others were life-threatening rights of passage.

"I remember getting into a big fight," says Officer Mary Brick. "I don't remember if the suspect was mental or on drugs or both, but he had just broken his mother's arm and his brother was wrestling with him out on the sidewalk. Two cars responded to the call. We arrived almost simultaneously on opposite ends of the street, and ran toward the fight that was still going on between the brothers. I don't remember how we determined who the bad guy was because they were two brothers fighting, but I dived onto the suspect's legs and tried to control him. He had steel-toed boots on and he kicked me in the head. I was not even aware of getting kicked at the time. I remember being blown backwards and immediately returning to the fray. I wrapped myself around the guy's legs because the brother and the other officers were dealing with his arms and upper torso. I just held on for dear life.

"Later, after we had gotten the guy subdued and he had been taken off in an ambulance with restraints, we went to a local restaurant to have coffee. My partner looked at me and said, 'Are you okay?' I was still feeling all pumped up and I said, 'Yeah, I'm fine. Why?' He said, 'Cause you've got a huge goose egg on your head.' I looked in a mirror and, sure enough, I had a big knot on my forehead from where I'd been kicked. But the adrenalin was just so powerful that I hadn't really realized what had happened until the officer mentioned it to me. And then my bruise started hurting.

"My brother was doing a ride along with me at the time," she adds, "and I had told him that if anything happened on my shift he could not interfere. So he watched the fight from the car. He said it was one of the hardest things he'd ever had to do in his life. He knew and trusted that I had training and the capability to handle myself, but he wanted so badly to get in and help me."

For First Niner Leslie Baranzini, her test of courage came two years after she joined the Seattle Police Department, when she and her partner responded to an early morning call about a woman brandishing a gun at the YMCA.

"My partner and I drove around until we saw the woman walking down the street," Baranzini recalls. "We were told she was armed so when I got out, I drew my gun and told her to take her hands out of her pockets slowly, while my partner went around the corner and parked and came at her from the rear. When I first pulled my gun, I was not even a bus length away from her. All of a sudden, she just started running towards me. Her hands came out of her pockets and all I saw were clenched fists. I did not see a gun, I did not see a knife, and so I thought, *This woman is not armed so I should re-holster.* So I re-holstered and the fight was on. It was a big fight. A plainclothes officer arrived on the scene and we finally got her down.

"Once the woman was under control, the plain clothes officer grabbed me, pushed me down and said, 'You're bleeding.' I just looked at him like he was nuts. How can I be bleeding from clenched fists? But she had a short knife in her clenched fist and she had stabbed me in the chest and in the back. I saw my blood was going squirt, squirt, squirt.

"The other officers ran to the trunks of their cars but they had no first aid kits. So I put pressure on my own wound. I said, 'I have a tampon in my pants pocket. Just reach in, get it, open it up, and it will make a nice compress.' The plain clothes officer said, 'I can't reach in your pants pocket.' I sat there thinking, *This isn't a sexual thing here.* I told him, 'Just reach in my pocket and pull it out!' Eventually the officer pulled the tampon out and used it to slow my bleeding."

Baranzini was rushed to Harborview Medical Center where she learned she had torn tendons and ligaments in her wrist and had received numerous knife nicks. Most of the wounds were minor, but the one stab wound in her chest missed her heart by a quarter of an inch.

"It just happened so fast," she says. "When the fight is on, your adrenalin starts flowing and you just have to take care of things. I never felt the knife go in.

"After everything had calmed down and I was resting in the hospital, I had time to think. It was my first week back on the job after having my daughter, and she was only six months old. I remember sitting back and wondering, *What would have happened to my daughter if I had been killed?*"

Like Baranzini, Sergeant Carol Minakami suffered a serious injury early in her career. Indeed, one year after she joined the department, she became the first female officer in Washington State to be shot in the line of duty.

"We were investigating a vehicle prowl call, and acting like typical cops," she recalls. "We were not paying any attention because juveniles are usually the ones who are involved in car prowls, and they either run when you show up or they're already gone."

Minakami and her partner drove into a particularly dark parking lot and discovered one of the cars had its doors wide open. They didn't see any teenagers around and assumed they had run off, but the prowler was actually a grown man who was hiding in front of the car. The officers pulled up, and Minakami got out of their patrol car to investigate.

"As I started walking toward the prowled car, the suspect just came over the hood and, BOOM, he shot me.

"I went down in the middle of the parking lot. An officer came up behind me and started firing back, and there was a huge gunfight. All I could hear were bullets flying overhead. I thought I was in the middle of Vietnam. I had no idea where the bad guy had gone. So I just stayed low and didn't stick my head up. No other officers got hurt and the shooter survived, despite being shot nine times."

Later, Minakami learned the prowler had murdered another woman several days before. He opened fire on her and the other officers because he mistakenly thought they were looking for him.

"I remember that as I lay there on the ground, my first thought was, *Thank God I was shot in the leg*," Minakami notes. "Being a woman out with a bunch of men, I was thinking that if I had been shot in the chest they would have to take my shirt off in the middle of the parking lot. As it turned out, the bullet struck me just below the knee and it put a huge hole through the pant leg. I used to joke and say, 'That really sucks. It was the only pair of pants that fit right, and now they're ruined.'

"I also remember thinking that somehow I had to prove something for womankind," she adds. "I put pressure on myself to prove that being shot wasn't going to slow me down so that all these men wouldn't say, 'Yeah, women are a bunch of wimps, and they can't handle the job.' So I pushed myself and went back to work way before I should have. I really felt that as the first woman shot in the state, all eyes would be on me to see how well a woman could handle it. I was having flashbacks and nightmares, but I pushed myself to go back on light duty about a month after I got shot, and I was back on the street a few months after that. I came back way before I should have, and I worked through the flashbacks and nightmares by myself. But I tell you now, twenty years later, I've been around long enough that I know better. I should have sat on a hot, sandy beach for three years."

"DINE-AND-DASH"

In the early hours of a cold December day in 1984, officer Nick Davis faced off against a petty thief, and all of the Seattle Police Department learned the hard truth that a life can be lost over the cost of an unpaid breakfast. Detective Linda Lane, one of the officers involved that tragic morning, remembers the incident as series of images strung together by calls over the police radio.

"It was First Watch hours, around 6 a.m.," Lane recalls quietly. "I was in my district and had made a traffic stop of a suspicious-looking vehicle when the call came out over the radio that Nick was going to the International House of Pancakes at 12th and Madison. A bunch of us were going there to join him for coffee."

The thirty-nine-year-old Davis was the effective center of a small group of officers nicknamed *The Gang of Six* who worked on the same squad and were fast friends. As the "gentle old giant" of the group, he often put out the call to get together mid-shift for a coffee break. Lane and the others always responded.

On this particular morning, however, Davis arrived at the pancake house ahead of the rest of the gang. When he walked into the restaurant, a young waiter asked him to catch a man who had done a "dine-and-dash" — left without paying the tab for his cheese blintzes breakfast.

"Nick took the waiter with him and they drove around the neighborhood looking for the guy," Lane explains. "Over the radio, you heard him say he saw the man in a parking lot a few blocks from the restaurant. Nick said he was going to approach the man and have a talk with him."

Davis drove over to the suspect—later identified as thirty-three-year-old Michael R. Trott—and explained that he knew the man had left the IHOP without paying for his meal. Trott replied that he was going to his own car to get money, and then turned and walked away. Undaunted, Davis again pulled alongside Trott.

"Nick started to step out of the patrol car while radioing for backup," Lane says. "Then, over the radio, I heard a panicked voice say: 'Help the officer!' and then the mike was suddenly torn out. I immediately got rid of my traffic stop, and jumped into my car."

While she was en route, Trott grabbed Davis and pulled him out of the squad car. The two men grappled, and then Trott threw the officer to the ground.

"Nick was a pretty big guy, probably about 5'11" and 275," Lane continues, "but the suspect was a huge football player, maybe 6'3" and 300 pounds. Nick was trying to get free, but the guy grabbed Nick's gun from his holster and shot him. Nick didn't have his vest on. He got the suspect off of him and tried to get away from him, but the guy shot him again. The waiter, just a kid, saw all of this because he had gotten out of the patrol car and was standing on the other side of the car. Nick had told the waiter to get out of there."

With the officer down, the waiter ran behind the patrol car and tried to stay out of sight. Trott started to walk around the front of the car, then suddenly turned and ran off with the officer's gun still in his hand.

"Two other officers and I arrived at the scene just about the same time," Lane notes. "Nick was lying on the ground bleeding from a gunshot wound to his chest.

"It is all so fuzzy now, and it was fuzzy then too," she adds. "But I remember two of us were doing CPR, while another officer called for Fire. After what seemed like a really long time, Fire got there. They were just over on 14th so you know they got there fast, but everything moved along just like they say — in slow motion.

"Dick Samaonski was doing mouth to mouth, Dennis was doing the compressions, and I was holding Nick's head back and his neck up so we could keep an airway open. He was unconscious, and gurgling. We found out later that even if he had been at the Harborview Medical Center trauma unit they couldn't have helped him because the bullet had severed his aorta. He was already basically dead by the time we were trying to revive him."

Another responding officer saw the shooter run away and followed him to a nearby club. Trott was discovered hiding in a back bathroom and was arrested. Later in court, he was found not guilty by reason of insanity.

"So he didn't pay the ultimate price for killing Nick," Lane says in a tone of disbelief. "All for a breakfast that cost $4.55."

There were other ironies. One was that Davis's wife also worked for the SPD as a 911 operator. Fortunately, that night she was off duty. Another was that Davis had switched to the graveyard shift (3:30 a.m. to 11:30 a.m.) four months earlier because he said he needed a change.

Even now, more than twenty years later, Lane remains haunted by that early December morning, and the loss of her comrade and friend.

"There have been instances in my career that I think have helped to make me a deeper-feeling person and more fiercely loyal to my comrades," Lane reflects. "The shooting of Nick Davis was one such incident. It was the first time I had ever seen anyone die like that. I'd been to car accidents and I'd even seen decapitated heads after the fact, but nothing I'd seen prepared me for seeing someone you know die right in front of you and not being able to do one goddamned thing about it."

~Photos~

Young Lis Eddy. Early 1980s.

Daljit Gill, the first East Indian officer on the Seattle Police Dept. 2008

Asst. Chief Noreen Skagen   1980s

Policewoman Sylvia Hunsicker modeling her self-made uniform. 1920s

Helen Karas (right) and Lillian Mitchell, the department's first African American policewoman. 1950s

Helen Karas (left) and Karen Ejde (right) with police communications officer. 1955

The Women's Bureau, 1955. Captain Irene Durham (front left) and Sergeant Kay Twohig. (front right)

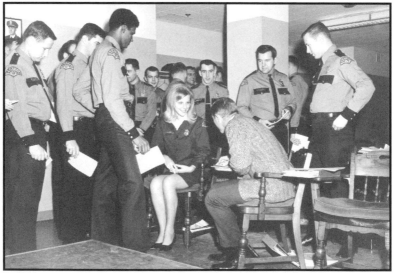

Policewoman Marlynn McLaughlin talking with celebrity Martin Milner of the television series, *Adam 12*. McLaughlin was the last policewoman hired before the Women's Bureau was disbanded in 1969.

Fresh out on the streets: Police officer Vicky Burt (Cauthorn) frisking a suspect. 1975

Police officer Toni Malliet in a publicity pose for the department. 1978

Joanne Hunt, the first female to serve as lieutenant of the Motorcycle Squad. 1987

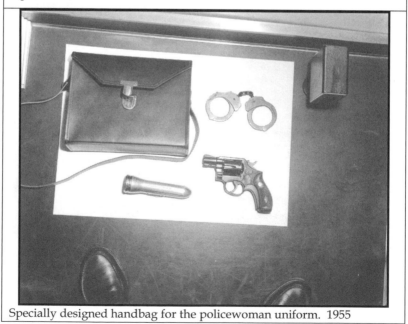

Specially designed handbag for the policewoman uniform. 1955

Helan Karas receives the "National
Police Officer of the Month" award
from Master Detective Magazine. 1968.

Phyllis Covington and Elvis
Presley, 1955

Helen Karas & Karen Ejde in
retirement 2000.

Sgt. Lis Eddy 2008

7
FITTING IN

As the number of female patrol officers continued to increase, so too did the obstacles to their success. One concerned an actual physical barrier, while another involved the walls that women often place between each other. And, as the First Niners started to move up the chain of command, they encountered the legendary "glass ceiling" and realized they were outsiders on the inside of the ultimate white male's club.

FACING "THE WALL"

"At the academy, I had the feeling the men were just kind of sitting there watching us, seeing what we could do," explains Sergeant Carol Minakami. "There were some men who would say, 'Ah, damn women...' and there was nothing you could ever do to make them accept you. But most of the guys just sat by and watched. I didn't want exceptions made for me. When I was told to get down and do fifty pushups, I got down and did fifty pushups, and the men started to think I was okay. I didn't say, 'I'm a girl and I can't do pushups.' But a lot of women walked in with the attitude, 'I'm a woman so you should make exceptions for me.' And the men resented them."

Minakami was not the only female recruit who eagerly got down and did pushups upon command, and most women successfully made it through the physical training at the academy. However, others struggled. One particularly difficult challenge for even those in great shape was "The Wall," a six-foot-tall structure that cadets had to scale.

"Oh, I hated The Wall," laughs Lieutenant Joanne Hunt. "Although I was physically fit from being a diver, and underwater I can move, on the surface I am kind of clumsy. Also, I have a disproportionately long torso and short legs, and I probably move like a duck. I could not get the technique to get over The Wall. I remember my physical training ("P.T.") instructor saying, 'Duffy!' — my maiden name — 'Get your butt over that wall!' The only thing that saved me was I had enough upper body strength to drag myself over the top."

"I had a lot of problems with The Wall on the first day of P.T.," notes Officer Tammy McClincy, who signed on in 1985. "The instructor took us out there and said, 'Okay, everybody over The Wall.' I looked at it and thought, *How am I going to get over that?* I watched everybody else do it and I thought, *Okay, I've got this down.* Then I ran up to The Wall and I went BLAM! I flattened right into it. Oh, god, it was embarrassing. The instructor told me, 'You just don't have the technique, but you can learn it.' So throughout the academy he worked with me. I was out there everyday. It took me time, but once I got the technique I was fine."

"I ran right up and jumped over it," the taller Officer Vicky Burt recalls. "But some of the women had problems with it. I remember we helped one of the women over The Wall at the tail end of the academy, and the instructors turned their backs. I don't know if the instructors turned their backs on purpose, but she passed and she made it onto the department."

"The Wall was hard for me too, but not for the usual reason," adds Detective Linda Lane. "What made it and the rest of the physical training tough was that two weeks into the Academy, I broke my right hand playing coed dodge ball. They were going to terminate me because of my broken hand, but I told them, 'Look, I didn't come all the way out here from Ohio just to get terminated and go back. So while everybody else is doing pushups, I'll do sit-ups, I'll run, I'll do whatever I have to do to stay and make it through this.' And that's what I did. The Seattle Police Department folks helped me and, with the cast on my hand, I typed my notes, I wrote, I took everything down that needed to be taken down, and then after class, we stayed and worked on the physical requirements. We worked The Wall so I learned to run and jump and place my foot just the right height so I could put my arm over the top. The back of the cast would catch over the top and that helped me get a grip to pull the rest of myself over. It hurt like hell, but I was determined to make it. There was no way I was going to get bombed out or quit."

"When I was an instructor at the academy I realized that a lot of women could not get over that wall because they just didn't have the upper body strength to climb it," notes Minakami. "The rumblings began and we started hearing, 'Get rid of The Wall because the women can't do it and we need to have a certain percentage of women to fill our quota.' What the administration should have been saying was, 'Listen, this is the standard. We'll help you meet it, but this is the standard.'

"To be fair, some men complained about The Wall too. But it really amazed me how many women wanted an excuse for being a woman. They'd say, 'I can't make it over The Wall.' I'd respond by telling them to start doing pull-ups and pushups to improve their upper body strength. But many of them wouldn't do it. They wanted the secret. In this day and age, I think there are a lot of people who, instead of working for something, want 'the secret.' Well, the only secret is that you have to work at it."

Despite some supporters, in 1989 the Seattle Police Department removed The Wall as a physical fitness requirement at the academy. Minakami believes that was a mistake.

"When I taught at the academy, I thought it needed to be there," she explains. "The Wall was an important part of physical training because officers never know when they're going to have to scale a wall to get out of harm's way, to chase the bad guys, to go help somebody. It helped develop the upper body strength you'd need to pull your partner out of danger if he or she got hurt. I remember one male student coming back to me and saying, 'You know, I never knew why the hell we had to go over this wall all the time. I thought it was the stupidest thing until one night I was in the back yard of a house, and I was crouched down in a corner watching the house. I looked up and there was a guy in the window with a gun, and I never went over a wall faster than I did then to get out of there.'

"By removing The Wall I think they took away something that was very important for officer safety, whether you're a male or female. They also removed any type of physical fitness requirement. There was a big fight to get rid of the standard because a lot of people couldn't meet it. For quite a few years, they had no physical fitness training or standard. Then they came up with a rule that you had to pass certain physical requirements to get into the academy, but then once you were in, there was no physical fitness training whatsoever other than self-defense tactics. There was no running, or similar training. I see that as a form of affirmative action, and I believe it is just basically telling people, 'You can't compete, so we have to lower our standards so you can make it.' I resent that attitude."

Although The Wall is no longer a part of academy training, the department has since equalized the physical training requirements for men and women.

"During the hiring phase they used to have a physical that was geared for women, but that has changed," says Officer Megan Bruneau, who joined the force in 2006. "Men and women now have to do the same physical tests and have to answer the same questions on oral boards. And at the academy, women used to do push-ups from their knees. No longer. They have to do the same number of push-ups as the men in the same way. You have to be four inches off the ground and you can't be sagging. They have to be the perfect push-ups. Men and women alike are judged on a scale. For push-ups, you have to do a minimum of twenty-one and a maximum of thirty-five. And you have to do between twenty-eight and thirty-eight sit-ups. There is also a mile-and-a-half run and a three-hundred-meter sprint. You can get different scores on individual requirements but overall you have to get a certain percentage. You can't get all minimums on everything or you fail. In the academy, everybody now does the same thing."

THE QUEEN BEE SYNDROME

Most of the women who joined the ranks of the Seattle Police Department in the late 1970s and early '80s were not surprised when male officers gave them the cold shoulder. What they didn't expect, however, was that some female officers who were already on the department also seemed unhappy to have them arrive. Indeed, many times the male officers proved more supportive.

"When you're a woman, you sometimes get nailed both ways," says Sergeant Carol Minakami. "Maybe some guy doesn't want you there because you're a woman, and some woman doesn't want you there because you're a woman. I saw it more in the beginning when I first came on the department. It was like some women didn't want other women to do well. I guess it was a little about territorialism, but it was also about how if all the other women didn't do well it would make them look better. There was no real sisterhood, no sense that 'Gee, I've been here a while, so let me help you along.' When you came on, you were pretty much alone."

"When I first came on in 1980, there were two groups of women on the department," notes Captain Wanda Barkley. "There were the ones who came on three years ahead of me in that first patrol wave, and then there were the women from the old Women's Bureau who had been around for ten to fifteen years. The two groups of women did not associate with one another. It was like we were back in high school with the seniors snickering at freshmen in the hallways and saying, 'Let's not acknowledge them or talk to them, and if they say "Hi," let's not say "Hi" back.' That's what some of the more senior women were doing on the department. And if you happened to be assigned to a squad where there was already a woman, oftentimes that woman became very competitive and the men then became *her* officers, not your officers. I was twenty-one at the time and it was all very weird."

Perception often depends on who is doing the perceiving and, indeed, that weirdness existed for all of the women, not just the new arrivals. Policewomen from the Women's Bureau era, for instance, felt equally ignored by the young women coming on.

"At the beginning, the new female patrol officers didn't want to have anything to do with us," recalls former policewoman turned Sergeant Mary Robinson. "All of us collectively and individually approached them and said, 'We'd be very happy to talk to you. Let us know if we can help.' Most of them didn't want it. Later, after time, they became a little more receptive. I think they thought we didn't know anything about what they were doing. I don't think that was fair. To be sure we hadn't done a lot of the street work, but we worked with a lot of people who did, we were out in the cars and we worked with the men. We had to learn the same laws, we had to pass the same academy. I have a hunch it was more their wish to distance themselves from us so that they didn't dare appear to be a part of the old guard in a new system, but that's just my assessment of it."

"We tried to get together with them once in a while for lunch," adds Major Beryl Thompson, "not to push any particular thoughts on them but to say, 'We're here, we've been here for a while, is there anything we can help you with?' But some of them had the attitude that 'My badge is just as big as yours and I have this and I have that and I have the police guild, and I really don't need you old folks.' They didn't say that directly, but that was the feeling I got. Most of them had no sense of history in terms of recognizing what it was like ten to fifteen years prior to their coming on, or what the women had gone through to get to where they were at that time."

Whether they hired on during the policewomen era or after female patrol officers hit the streets, all of the women seem to agree that females frequently don't share the sense of camaraderie that men often enjoy.

"Women don't end up being the best moral and emotional support for other women," suggests Detective Linda Patrick. "My friends and I have discussed this and we call it the 'Queen Bee' syndrome. When women start working in a male-dominated environment they want to be accepted and they kind of become one of the guys. If you become one of the guys you take on a lot of the same attitudes, and if another female comes along it's almost like the first woman has a territory, this position to protect. They don't give you any kind of support at all and, if anything, they feel threatened. Not by you personally, but by the fear that you might do something that could be perceived as weak, or something that would give females a bad reputation because people are always waiting and anticipating for a female to mess up so they can say, 'See, you really don't belong here.'

"What they were trying to protect was the image that women could cut it. If you're already there and you've already cut it, you don't want someone to come in and screw it up because the action of one female can destroy all female officers' reputations for five or ten years. It's the same idea when nationally the actions of one police officer can affect all. Like with Rodney King. The actions of those few officers in Los Angeles affected all of us, and we ended up paying for it for a long time. Well, if the actions of one woman were perceived as proof she couldn't cut the job, then every woman would be perceived the same, whether they were there doing their jobs or not. And then everyone would have to start over proving themselves from scratch."

"When I came on, the women on the department were more of the 'stand back and watch' types," notes Officer Jennifer McLean, who joined in 1986. "In fact, when I was first assigned to a precinct, the guys were much more outgoing and willing to help, but I did not find the women to be at all friendly. No words said, no exchanges about how the job goes, no guidance about how you should handle yourselves in certain situations. Later on, I talked to a few officers and they said they felt very threatened. It was more like, 'I'm used to being the queen bee in my squad with these guys and here comes another person, and she threatens my position on the squad.'

"I'm talking about the women who were the trailblazers in patrol," she adds. "I don't hold any judgment against them because I think their pathway was so much more difficult than mine. It was more like what my mom faced when she was entering the business world years earlier and had to deal with those kinds of roadblocks. The women who came onto the department in the 1970s were the ones who pushed down the barriers, who faced horrible doubt from police officers, their wives, and citizens who said they couldn't do the job. I benefited from all the bullshit they had to go through."

Although many of the women attribute the queen bee syndrome to the pressures of trying to fit in to a male-dominated profession, others suggest this tension may simply be due to how women often relate to each other.

"Women sometimes can be their own worst enemies," notes Officer Marlynn McLaughlin. "We should have a network on the department to help new women get comfortable with things, but we don't. It's the nature of women. The women in any field will tell you that. We are worse than men sometimes. I don't know why. It just is, and it's too bad. They're territorial in some respects, or jealous of their positions. I didn't see that in the Women's Bureau. The majority of women there were great to us when we came on, and they did whatever they could to help us out."

"Actually, I think a lot of what the cold-shouldering rookies experienced had more to do with their newness on the street than any particular agenda," says Sergeant Lis Eddy. "When I first came on, new officers — male and female — weren't really spoken to. If you talk to guys who have been on twenty years now, they'll tell you, 'Yeah, when I came on my partner said, 'Your job is to sit in the car and shut up.' Nobody ever said that to me, but I can remember knowing when I came on that there was this unwritten rule that you didn't talk to senior officers until they had talked to you first. Like in the locker room, you might say hello if you passed them going in or out, but you didn't really initiate conversation with them. My experience was, some of the veteran women who had two or three years on would not speak to me. But then, some of them did, and some of those people are my friends today. They were friendly women who were nice to me and offered me help."

For her part, Eddy was pleased when another female officer was assigned to her precinct and on the same watch.

"I was the only woman in my squad for a while," she explains, "and when Diane Stone came to Second Watch I begged her to come into the squad. I wasn't threatened by her at all. I wanted her because it would be more fun to have another woman on the squad. I got along very well with the guys, but I wanted Diane's companionship and her friendship.

"Being the only woman on the squad was hard sometimes. I found it really awkward when there you are, your whole squad is male besides you, and they would start discussing women's breasts. You'd think to yourself, *Well, this is real interesting to me. What am I supposed to say here? I can't participate in this conversation.* And sometimes you'd have a male partner who, as you drove down the street, would say, 'OOOH, look at the hooters on her.' It was uncomfortable. What are you supposed to say, 'Yeah, man, she really has a pair?' I always thought that was stupid. It wasn't offensive to me — it was just tacky. I always wanted to throw it back at him, to say something like, 'Wow! Look at the bread basket on that guy!' "

Even today, some women say the queen bee Syndrome remains a reality.

"Female officers can be really catty with each other," explains one officer who requested anonymity because she recently joined the department, and she fears repercussions from her coworkers if she speaks on the record. "Police work is unique because it is such a male-dominated profession and the women are competing with each other. We're trying to prove to everyone that we're competent, and there can be a lot of scratching out the eyes of other women to get there. Women are our biggest critics. We are harder on each other than any of the men on the department.

"The Queen Bee syndrome still exists. That's part of the cattiness big time. The guys will be welcoming, but the one female won't give eye contact, or will be really short with you, or you'll hear her saying really catty things. It's ridiculous. Instead of being excited that there's another woman around it becomes very competitive. Not everyone. There are a lot of really great supportive women, but there are also enough of the Queen Bees that they really stand out. They treat everyone like that, so it's not like they are inconsistent. Sometimes some of the male officers will comment on how harsh female police officers can be to each other. I was lucky to find a group of women at my precinct who are supportive of each other. We're grateful that we've found each other, and we've often commented to each other on how rare such camaraderie is among women on the department."

MOVING UP THE CHAIN OF COMMAND

Many female officers first became interested in police work during or after college when they realized that the starting pay

was considerably higher than that of other occupations. Captain
Wanda Barkley was different. For her, the desire to fight crime
came at the tender age of twelve when, while viewing the
television series *The FBI* starring Efrem Zimbalist, Jr., she
suddenly realized she wanted to be an agent.

"When I watched *The FBI* I liked that they were able to help
people," Barkley explains, "and that they were able to stop
injustices or prevent people from taking advantage of others. Of
course, the reality is that the impact you're going to have is fairly
limited, but I think almost every police officer comes to the job
with some view that they are going to help society and set right
the wrongs that they see."

Stopping the injustices of the world appeared easy at first —
after all, all of the problems on television were solved within
minutes — but Barkley quickly learned her dream job might be
beyond her reach. While the men of *The FBI* seemed to have no
difficulty catching the criminals, they were alone because in the
early 1970s there were no female G-Men.

"When I was thirteen or fourteen I looked up the FBI
application and women were not allowed in the FBI," she recalls.
"I talked with my mother and said, 'Wait a minute, I can't do
this. Why can't they allow women in?' Her view was optimistic.
She said, 'By the time you turn twenty-three or twenty-four, it
will have changed, so don't worry about it.' My mother was six
feet tall, and she was always the kind of person who said, 'You
can do whatever you want.' She had served as a lieutenant in the
Navy WAVE program during World War II. The
groundbreaking she did during that time served as my best role
model."

After graduating from high school, Barkley went to college
to study law enforcement. By that time, the FBI's policies had
indeed changed to allow women, but the organization wouldn't
hire anyone under the age of twenty-three. Eager for experience,
she worked first with the University of Washington Police

Department while still in college, and then hired on to the Seattle Police Department in 1980 at the age of twenty-one, making her one of the youngest officers on the department.

"Because I was twenty-one but looked sixteen, I had a lot of people go, 'This is a joke, right? You're a *cadet*.' I'd respond, 'No, they don't hand out handguns to cadets, thank you very much.' 'Really, you've got to be sixteen.' 'NO, I'm *twenty-one*!' "

Barkley's age and youthful looks continued to create challenges for her as she moved up the chain of command. Frequently, she was the youngest of her rank on the department. When she became captain at the age of thirty-eight, she was the youngest woman to ever achieve that rank at the Seattle Police Department. Each step upward required a different mindset from the last.

"When I was a new sergeant going into patrol," Barkley notes, "I had been at a desk job for two-and-a-half years, and I was concerned about how to introduce myself to the members of my new squad. I talked to a lieutenant about my concerns, and he said, 'If you want to make an impression on them, ride your Harley to work the first night. It will give them something to talk to you about, and it will set with them an image of you.' So I rode my Harley in, and people were asking, 'Whose Harley is that?' Officers came up to me to talk about what model it was and how long I'd had it, and to tell me about their motorcycles. I think I rode my bike to work only once or twice, but it broke the ice with my squad. It was one of the best pieces of advice I'd ever received.

"The jump from sergeant to lieutenant is a tremendous change in mindset," she continues. "As a sergeant you have to look after the needs of your officers, but as a lieutenant you need to start thinking about the needs of the department. When you're on the street as a sergeant, it's like playing checkers. You think, *Okay, that person on the street who just ran around that corner is probably dealing drugs. We better arrest him.* It's relatively straight forward. When you're a lieutenant, however, your job becomes a game of chess.

You have to think about what impact your actions will have on the department. Or you have to wonder, why is City Council asking this question? Why is the Chief's office asking for that? If I take this step, will it put the department in a bad light? It requires a lot more of a political mindset of looking at the good of the department and the good of the citizens above all else."

For Barkley, the transition to captain was the most dramatic shift because it changed her whole perspective on what it means to be a police officer.

"Police work on the officer level gives you instant gratification," she explains. "Every day, you lock bad guys up, give support to the victims, and provide immediate services, both positive and negative. But as you move up the ranks, your job is to create an environment in which officers can do their jobs, which is considerably different because it requires influencing a lot of people to do positive work, so the officers can do their work in a positive manner. As you go up higher, and I do like being captain, the politics become incredibly difficult. That's fine, but the number of people you associate with becomes smaller, and the number of people you have to convince that this is a good idea is fewer because there are only six assistant chiefs.

"And, as the politics with the upper brass becomes more complex, so do the politics with the officers below. Often the women officers in particular expect their female superiors to always be on their side. They may want me to ride in on a big white horse and say, 'I'm going to take up your cause and run forward with it.' Most of the time I've gone to bat for women who I felt were being treated differently and found they were being judged more stringently than the men. But sometimes I may end up saying, 'I think your cause is not one that needs to be fought.' Or I may realize I won't be able to resolve their problem.

"Let's say someone believes she didn't get a position because of gender bias," Barkley says. "She complains to you and asks you to help her. So you make a phone call and you discover that there were three women in contention for the job, and one of the other women got it. You also learn this person didn't get the job because she lacked the experience, she didn't do the necessary training, or she did not put herself in the position where she could get it. Then you have to go back and say, 'Hey, I've got to tell you that you weren't the most qualified. These are some of the things you need to do to make yourself more qualified.' In the split second of the original moment, you're going to look like you're backing up the old system."

Regardless of where women are in the chain of command, Barkley believes they often struggle in their rise to the top because they don't have the right frame of reference.

"One of the biggest detrimental hurdles for women and people of color is learning the game," Barkley offers. "Not necessarily deciding to play the game, but understanding what the rules are and what plays well or not. Without having that passed on, you're out of the game before you even know one is being played. I know a number of women who have fallen from promotional tracks or have not gotten assignments, not based upon their gender, but based upon what they've done and on how they present themselves. Some women have chosen to take some very strong stands on minor issues, and I take my hat off to them. But it is oftentimes difficult to balance that with getting a reputation of being this person who's so prickly that you can't get close to him or her.

"It's not a matter of presenting yourself as a man as much as understanding the game. There's a point at which in your process, as you come onto this department, you want to become one of the guys to fit in. Some women do this by starting to talk like a truck driver, telling dirty jokes with the best of them. Well, as you move up in command, this kind of personality doesn't play well. Women who move up have to adjust and change from being one of the guys to being more professional. Some of the women don't realize this, however, and get frustrated when they don't move forward.

A lot of times the guys they're imitating also aren't moving forward.

"As one now-retired major told me, 'You will go far in this department because you think like a man and you are someone who we can understand better than one of those people who is more radical.' I didn't take that as a compliment. At that moment the issue was not that I was male or female, but whether I was someone they felt comfortable with allowing me into a place where I could potentially have power."

Barkley and other women admit that females moving up the chain of command frequently experience feelings of isolation and extreme pressure to perform.

"When I came up through the ranks, there weren't a lot of women in higher positions who thought about providing support," notes Lieutenant Debie King. "They were too busy fighting for their careers. When you're breaking new ground you don't have a whole lot of time to reach back and offer help. Later on, when these women got to where they were going to go and felt comfortable with where they were and with themselves, then they did reach back. I'm talking about Pat Lamphere, and Beryl Thompson and Noreen Skagen, the women who really had to break the mold.

"When you move up the ranks, there is a tremendous amount of pressure on you because you're different from most of the other command staff," she adds. "Instead of coming to work and being a guy and getting away with providing sixty-five to seventy percent work output, most of us feel like we have to do 120 percent minimum. Now, the idea that men can get away with seventy percent is part perception and part reality, and I'm not saying this situation is specific to the police department. I think it's whenever there's somebody different who is breaking that glass ceiling. They always feel they have to run the race harder and longer than anybody else. You feel you've got more obstacles to overcome and have more to prove than anybody else. And I think when you bring women into a predominantly male organization, the women are always going to feel that expectation of performance, whether it's reality or not."

"Even now, I think I have to do a little better than the guys to be considered half as good," agrees Assistant Chief Cindy Caldwell. "I think in command it's even worse. We've had a few things happen that show guys don't accept women's authority. They will tolerate a male supervisor or commander who's not very good, but a woman can be really good at most things, and if she's not good at one thing, they'll all just jump on it. Let's say this woman is really bright and knows what she's doing, but she doesn't quite treat the egos the right way or doesn't smile enough. Her superiors will ask her, 'How come you're not smiling?' Well, we have guys who don't have interpersonal skills, and no one asks them to smile and be pleasant and sweet and charming.

"If you're not careful, you start to personalize your experience based on your gender, your race, your orientation, or whatever else there is that makes you unique, and you don't ever really know what others are experiencing. I don't know what white males experience, for instance, or males in general. I do know that over time you do develop a reputation which, if it is a good one, allows you to make mistakes occasionally. Or you can sometimes not be at the top of your game and people will give you latitude. It's just a matter of how you've spent your career working. But, regardless of your reputation, you never stop having to prove yourself as a woman. That's the reality."

Barkley adds, "I would guess that after a certain point, white males don't have to continue to prove themselves, but women and people of color always seem to have to keep proving themselves. That's what an assistant chief said to me four or five years ago. He said, 'Because you're a woman, you have to keep proving yourself. That's why we keep putting you in the hotspots, so you can continue to show you can do it.' I thought, It's great that I keep getting the tough assignments, but what happens when I keep proving myself and then I fail at something? Are they then going to say, 'See, we knew she couldn't do it?' Or, 'We knew a woman couldn't do it?' "

8
SURVIVAL STRATEGIES

"There were times when African Americans would try to appeal to my African American-ness to get me to cut them a break. Or they would say, 'I see you have that white boy in the car there with you and you have to impress him,' and I would respond, 'Oh, yeah, Master wants me to write you this ticket.' I would just be crazy and give it right back to them."
— Detective Linda Lane

For female cops, working the streets requires a wide range of survival strategies to deal with every aspect of police work, from defendants who are bigger than them to dead bodies at crime scenes. Some females carry themselves *with attitude* to cut off any would be challengers, while others develop a philosophy about police work that may involve a "shtick" for dealing with suspects. Officers who are gay have to learn how to handle the additional prejudices male coworkers and citizens have about lesbians. Ultimately, each woman develops her own unique way of dealing with the stresses that exist both out on the streets and inside the precincts.

SIZE DOES MATTER... SOMETIMES
"When I'm out in my uniform, people are afraid of me," notes Marlynn McLaughlin with only a slight laugh. "I'm 5'11" tall, and I go out with that vest on, carry a .357, wear black gloves, and carry myself with attitude. A lot of it is attitude. You talk to the other gals and they'll tell you—it is all how you walk into the room. Your presence. You can do a lot with that. If you walk in like you

know what you're doing, people will believe you know what you're doing. You have to take command."

One officer who doesn't have the luxury of height is diminutive Irene Lau, who joined in 1989. At 4'10" tall, she is the shortest patrol officer on the department.

"Everybody—men and women alike—always comment about how small I am," Lau explains, "and they often ask how can I do this job being so tiny. But I just let it go. Size is a legitimate concern, but you just have to take precautions."

"I don't blame the guys because I too am little," notes the 5'1" Sergeant Lis Eddy. "When I first saw Irene, I thought, *There's a tiny woman. She's smaller than me and I probably outweigh her by fifty pounds.* I felt probably the way men did when I came on. I saw her and I thought, *I'm not sure I want her backing me up because she looks like she could be hefted up and thrown at you.* I don't blame the fellows for wondering, *Geez, if I'm getting my butt kicked, can she do anything about it?* It would be the same if it were a small man."

Lau, whose sister is Washington state Court of Appeals Judge Linda Lau—famous for sentencing teacher Mary K. Letourneau for having an affair with a junior-high-school student—first got the notion of entering law enforcement when she met federal drug enforcement agents while working in China for various U.S. corporations. When she eventually returned to the States and put in an application with the Seattle Police Department, her size immediately became an issue.

"I was on the interview panel when Irene came on," Captain Malliet says. "She is truly one of the brightest people I have ever talked to in my entire life, and that came through during the interview. But all the men on the panel wanted to do was talk about her size. It was great to be there and to be able to say, 'What does her size have to do with whether she answered all the questions right or not? That's for her to worry about, not for us to worry about. We are on the oral board. These are the questions we posed to her. Did we like all of her responses? Yes, we did. So our job is to pass her on.' "

The oral board did indeed pass Lau on, she successfully completed all of the other tests and interviews, and she was hired. But the department remained uncertain of what to do with her once she passed the academy. While rookie officers normally are assigned to work with three different field training officers over a period of three months, Lau found herself bounced around from FTO to FTO, and from precinct to precinct, for more than four months. The department seemed determined to keep her in training indefinitely, but toward the end of her field training she was assigned to a squad that backed her for permanent assignment.

"The squad of guys that I got assigned to was great," Lau recalls. "They stood by me and helped me understand that size had nothing to do with being a good officer. For instance, there were days when I'd feel bad that I couldn't fight as well as the other guys on the squad, but they'd say, 'Irene, there's always going to be someone bigger than you no matter how tall you are, even if you're six feet tall. You just have to take the necessary precautions to take care of yourself.' So I have developed my own methods of officer safety, as all officers have to do.

"When I make contacts out on the street I always position my car so that it is between me and them, and I call the suspects over to me. I have them stay on one side of the car and I stay on my side of the car until my backup arrives. I also talk 'the talk' and stall. But if they choose to run away, I will chase them if the call warrants it.

"I work by myself and I go up against bruisers all the time," she adds, "so I've developed a theory about police work. My theory in a nutshell: I try to mother everyone. Guys may beat their wives, their lovers, their kids, whoever, but not many of them will raise their hands against their mother. And if they do, they're crazy, and you better bring the posse with you. So if I'm out there and I meet up with a big bruiser, I talk to him, mother him, and hopefully distract him long enough for the posse to get there."

Lau puts her theory to the test every day she is out on the streets, and so far she has been successful at avoiding major fights. In one close call, she was on patrol at two a.m. when she came upon a bare-chested man dragging a woman behind him.

"The woman was flat on her back and he was pulling her by the arms backwards down the sidewalk," Lau recalls. "Then he let go of her and he just started jumping up and down on her head, putting the boots to her. She was curled up in a fetal position. I saw this and immediately radioed it in but, of course, backup takes some time to respond, so I knew I had to do something to calm the guy down. He was so enraged that he didn't even see me pull up right next to him with all of my lights on.

"I got out and said, 'Hey, what are you guys doing tonight?' He said, 'My woman, she's trying to leave me. I want her to come home with me right now.' He started to pull her back up on her feet.

"I said, 'Hey, mellow out, this is Sunday, it's the Lord's Sabbath. You should be sitting at home having a roast in front of the fire with your family.'

"He dropped her again, and began this discourse with me. He said, 'I want her to come home with me right now, and she says she's going to leave me.'

"I told him, 'Hey, we can talk about this. Maybe I can help you work something out and maybe she will go home with you, okay, but let's just talk about this.' And it went on like that until my backup showed up. We grabbed him and took him away for felony assault. After the defendant was taken away, I was able to turn my attention to the victim, who was sobbing and still curled up on the sidewalk. The suspect was later convicted, and I received a note from the detective who followed the case. He wrote that the man probably would have killed his wife had I not intervened.

"Size is an issue no matter whether you're male or female," Lau concludes. "The name of the game is to stay alive and in one piece so you can go home at the end of your shift."

"When Irene came on the department," Sergeant Carol Minakami recalls, "I remember hearing rumors about her before she'd even hit the streets, things like that she was so short she couldn't pull the trigger of a gun. But you know what? She came out and did one helluva job. She was always willing to back other officers and to respond to calls. What I hear people saying about her now is that she's a good police officer. And she is. She probably had to fight harder to be a good police officer, and I don't take that away from her."

THE DOA QUEEN

Lieutenant Debie King joined the Seattle Police Department in 1977—first as a parking enforcement officer and then two years later as a police officer. When you meet Debie King, she reminds you of the actress Sally Field on a day when Ms. Field is feeling particularly perky. At fifty-seven, Lt. King is bright and enthusiastic, and she eagerly shares lively anecdotes from her days on the streets. She joined the force after eleven years of sales and managerial experience, and this background, plus her innate gift for gab, proved invaluable out on the streets.

"I've repeatedly told the department that they should be looking for people with sales experience," King explains. "After all, as police officers we are selling a product people have already paid for but hope to God they never have to use. When they call 911, it's like calling their insurance agent to file a claim because they have a big ding in their car. When I got here, I was a little surprised there wasn't more customer service going on. Out on the street, I always looked at citizens as the customer who really hated to have to call me, but when they did they expected some extraordinary service. That was my challenge always—to try to make them feel a little bit better about having called 911."

Besides calming an unsettled public, King also developed a way to charm people she was just about to place under arrest. A natural storyteller, she knew she needed her way with words because at a height of just under 5'5", she is not immediately intimidating.

"My ability to tell stories really helped on the streets," she explains. "There were numerous occasions where my backups were a long ways away, and I had to make multiple arrests. If you have three suspects, for instance, it's not safe to try to cuff them all, and generally I only had two pairs of cuffs on me anyway. So you have to hold all of them at bay until you get backup there, so you can do a proper search and cuff them. I used to tell suspects some really interesting tales, and very convincingly, about why they should be compliant.

"One very rainy night I got a call that three men were stealing firewood and other stuff from a supermarket. The three suspects had run down into an alley. I went down the dark alley and found them. They were bigger than me, and there were more of them than me. I had them cornered and told them to stand against the wall with their hands up. They complied, but my backup was going to take some time getting there and I had to find some way to hold them. They didn't want to stay, and they were upset because they had new dos that were getting ruined in the rain. They kept complaining and insisting they were going to leave.

"Finally I said, 'You know, I've just about had it with all of your complaining here. My backup is on the way, but until they get here you're going to stay up against this brick wall here, and you're going to do what I tell you. I need to get off work here in about twenty minutes, and it is imperative I get off on time tonight because I have a hot date with my TV.'

"They all go, 'What?'

I said, 'Yeah. *Dallas* comes on tonight, and I never miss it no matter what, because it is my favorite show. It's coming on in about forty-five minutes. I will admit to you that I made a fatal mistake today because I forgot to set my VCR, so I can't tape it. And as I told you before, I never miss one. So what I am suggesting to you guys is that you stay still, you make this as easy as possible until my backup gets here. If I were you, I wouldn't piss me off right now because I get real upset when I miss my favorite TV show.'

"The three men looked at me and said, 'What?' One said, 'I don't even believe this shit. This is the biggest crock I've ever heard.'

"We went on and on, and I engaged them in this incredible conversation about how important *Dallas* was to me. At the same time I kept reminding them to keep their hands away from their faces and against the wall. About seven or eight minutes later, my backup finally showed up. He knew I was at the end of my shift and he said, 'I'll take them from here because you need to go home.' And the three suspects went, 'Yeah, because she's only got twenty minutes until her favorite show.' One of them said, 'I am really glad he's taking us in because you are *crazy*.' "

King's ability to talk her way out of difficult situations proved particularly valuable when facing off the most dangerous criminals. One night she responded to a radio call at a check-cashing store where a man was attempting to pass stolen checks. With her backup delayed at another call, King arrived at the scene to find one very angry, very large suspect.

"He was pretty scary—probably 6'3" and 270-300 pounds," she recalls. "The people who ran the check-cashing place were so afraid of him that they were all in hiding. I started talking to the suspect, telling him why I was there and generally chatting with him to size him up as quickly as possible. I didn't know anything about him then except that he was a really big guy and that cashing stolen checks is a felony. But he wasn't real interested in talking to me, and he kept blowing me off.

"Finally, I said, 'Okay, enough. You've got two choices. This is A: You're going to turn around and be a nice guy and cooperate with me, I'm going to put the handcuffs on you, and we'll get this settled down at the station. Or we have B: you have committed a felony, and you're going to go in come hell or high water. I'm going to tell you right now, I'm not going to wrestle you because I'm too small to wrestle you.' I put my hand on my gun and I said, 'B is Bertha here, and I will shoot your ass. That's all there is to it. I'm not going to mess around.' "

"He looked at me for a moment and said, 'You can't do that.'

"I replied, 'Oh, yes I can, and I'll argue it after you're buried. I'm going to be tried by twelve, but you're going to be carried by six. And when the jury finds out how goddamned big you are and how small I am, and you're not going to be able to tell your side of the story, well, they're going to believe me. So what will it be, A or B?' I put my hand on my gun again and started to pull it out of the holster. And he said, 'A!'

"I put cuffs on him and put him in my car. My backup had still not arrived. Once in my car, I ran his name and found out he had a murder warrant out of Texas for killing his mother. He had tied her up, bludgeoned her, and taken her checks."

While talking to hardened criminals often required creativity and a dash of deception, King says dealing with troubled kids necessitated a much different approach—speaking the truth.

"People have soft spots, and kids are no exception," she notes. "Especially with young boys, I learned that if I could figure out where they were vulnerable, I could use those soft spots to try to reach them. And, if somehow I could get them to cry, then I knew that maybe, just maybe, they would listen to what I had to say.

"I remember one boy in particular whose mother had recently been divorced. When he was fifteen, the boy started running with a bad crowd and was causing all sorts of problems. I didn't know about him until one day I got a call that there was a burglary in progress involving kids breaking into a house. I went to the location and found this boy and his friends inside the home. When I ordered everyone down on the ground and told them to put their hands behind their backs, the other kids complied. But he wouldn't. He said he lived there, and he told me he didn't have to listen to me.

"He was standing in the shadows so I couldn't see his hands very well. He was also moving around a lot. Given the circumstances, I was very close to shooting him. Finally, I talked him into stepping into the light. I got cuffs on him, and took him down to the precinct. Later I learned we really were in his house, and that he and his friends were ripping off his own mother. I felt pretty shook up because I had been so close to shooting him.

"When I got him down to the precinct," King continues, "he was still real belligerent. I sat him down and I said, 'I need you to hear me for a minute. I don't think you're getting this. I was so close to *shooting you*. Do you understand what that means? I almost killed you in your own home. How do you think that would have made me and your mother feel? How dare you do that to me?' I was so upset I was trembling, and he saw it.

"I just kept grinding into him and, after a while, I started to see a little flicker in his eyes. I kept working him, and the next thing I knew, he was crying. I stepped out of the room, got a box of Kleenex, opened the door, threw it into the room, and then slammed the door and locked it. I walked away. I could hear him in there just balling his eyes out. After a little while, I stepped back into the room and said, 'Are you ready to talk?' He said yes, and we had a long discussion.

"No charges were pressed, but I had several more contacts with him and his mother throughout the months that followed, and I worked with his mother to get him some counseling. Every time the boy saw me, he would start shaking because he remembered the discussion we'd had. These days, I run into his mother every once in a while, and when she sees me she just lights up because that interaction changed her life—it changed his life.

He is grown up now, has kids of his own, and has become a successful person. That's one example of where I got someone to cry, and he started to listen."

King's most bizarre street encounter occurred when she received an early-morning radio call about someone shooting off a gun at a seedy motel in north Seattle. While the regular sector officer was dispatched to cover the front of the two-story building, King was sent to check out the back. As she pulled up to the motel, she saw a man lean out of a second story window with an assault rifle in his hands. The rifle was pointed directly at her.

"I slid my patrol car to a stop so my driver's side would be the farthest away from him, and I bailed out my door. I immediately got on the radio and told dispatch my situation. Once I finished my transmission, I crouched down behind the engine block and tried to peek around. I saw the guy drop his gun down onto the ground below the window. The next thing I knew, he was hanging out of the window, and he was completely naked."

As King continued to watch, the suspect jumped out and caught himself on the motel sign that hung off the side of the building.

"For a moment, he just dangled off the sign," she explains. "The gun was on the ground below him, and I knew that if he dropped down he would have access to the weapon. I thought, *I'm going to have to either fish or cut bait — either I stay here and face gunfire, or I rush in and hope I get to the rifle before he does.*

"The weapon was about fifty feet away from me, and there was no cover to protect me between my car and the rifle. It was just open sidewalk. I remember seeing tiny blades of grass in the cracks in the sidewalk and thinking, *Well, this certainly isn't going to cut it.*"

King decided to rush for the rifle. She stepped out from behind her patrol car with her own gun drawn and pointed at the naked suspect. At the same time, she ordered the man to remain absolutely still.

"Just as I stepped out, he dropped down from the motel sign and landed on his haunches like a monkey on the sidewalk, several feet away from where his rifle was laying. The gun was now within his reach. The guy was as white as a white shirt, and I thought I had a druggie on my hands. I screamed at him, 'Don't touch the gun! Leave the gun alone! Move away from the gun!'

"I kept moving towards him. The man was still crouched down on the sidewalk, and you could see his fingers slowly moving towards the weapon. I kept yelling, 'Don't do it. I *will* shoot you!' And I was fully prepared to shoot him because if he got to the rifle first he would nail me."

"As I continued to run toward him, I could see the hammer come back on my gun. I also saw his fingers shaking as he gradually moved towards the gun. By this point I was totally screaming at him: 'DON'T TOUCH THE GUN! STAND UP OR I WILL SHOOT YOU!' "

Despite King's warning, the naked man kept moving slowly toward his rifle. As she closed the distance between her and the suspect, he was only a matter of inches from grabbing the gun. Still, King did not fire.

"Finally, I said, 'Okay, that's it. I *am* going to shoot you.' And in one millisecond, I saw his fingers flinch just a hair backwards and that made me ease up on my trigger squeeze. By then I was still about ten feet from him. He then suddenly stood up and ran away, leaving his rifle on the sidewalk.

"I immediately ran after the man, passing the primary officer as he was walking around from the front of the motel. I dived onto the suspect, knocked him to the ground, and quickly got cuffs on him. The primary covered the man in a blanket, and we then searched the hotel to make certain the suspect was alone. Eventually, we learned that the man was high on drugs and had thought bad people were after him. In the motel he had fired off thirteen rounds, and had tried to shoot the toilet in his room. He was fortunate no one was injured, because one of the rounds went through into another room and just missed a kid's head."

Perhaps King's most challenging cases were ones involving people she couldn't talk to or convince to cooperate because they were already beyond help—they were dead.

"When someone becomes a police officer, they bring to the table a lot of issues that they have to grapple with," she notes. "One is, can you shoot somebody? The second is, how are you going to deal with death? As an officer you deal with it a lot, and you have to be a strong person. Many people are afraid of dead bodies, afraid somehow death will get them, too. It depends on how they were raised. When I grew up I was surrounded by old people—my grandfather, my aunts and uncles—and they were dropping like flies. For me, that made a big impression. And, back then in the early 1950s, they always had open-casket funerals. I experienced one of those as a child, and that was enough for me."

King's first professional experience with death occurred before she became a patrol officer during her days as a PEO (Parking Enforcement Officer)—a job that in other cities might be called a "meter maid."

"I was working downtown and this guy got off a bus at 4th and Virginia, and collapsed onto the sidewalk," she explains. "I heard on the radio that there was a man down. There was another PEO in the area and both of us went to try to help. He was probably in his late fifties or mid-sixties. When we got to him, he was unconscious and wasn't breathing, but he had a heart beat. We tried to resuscitate him, and then we lost the heartbeat and couldn't get it back. I was holding him at the time, and he died in my arms. Afterwards, everybody said, 'Well, you did your best.' But I kept thinking, *Gee, I should be able to work better magic than this.*

"The incident affected me greatly. At that time, I was in the process of applying to become a police officer, and I realized I needed to confront my own fears about dead people and dead bodies. I thought, *You've got to face these issues at some point. You can't figure them out on the street when you're an officer because you've got to be the all-knowing, all-seeing, can-do person that people expect of the police.*"

King decided to approach the PEO supervisor—Sergeant Pat Lamphere—and asked to be sent back through a first-aid class. Lamphere agreed, but recommended King also visit the medical examiner's office and watch some autopsies to help her get used to dead bodies.

"Several other people in the parking enforcement unit had similar concerns," King recalls, "and we all went up there and spent an entire day observing five autopsies. I don't mean from a gallery—we were standing right there looking into the body cavity. And the autopsies were pretty graphic. One guy had died from a motorcycle accident. Another lady had been killed in a car accident, and one of her legs was severed off. Then there was a young child who had died of child abuse, and a man who had stuck a shotgun in his mouth and blown his brains out. The medical examiner had no lack of bodies that day. Watching all the autopsies, I thought, *This is so incredible.* I could not believe how we are created, and how the inside of our bodies is a work of art. Everything is so perfectly placed and functional. It just boggled my mind. I walked away with a real positive feeling, and I knew that from that point forward I would be able to handle whatever I saw out on the street."

King didn't have to wait long. Soon after her visit to the medical examiner's office, the Seattle Police Department accepted her application to become a police officer and sent her through the academy. She hit the streets as a rookie officer in late 1980, and almost immediately received her first DOA (Dead On Arrival) call—on Halloween night!

"It was a very dark night," she recalls with a laugh. "The DOA was a woman recluse. The neighbor and his wife would take her food every once in a while. That night they went over to check on her, and knocked on her door. When they got no response, the man got into the house and found the woman dead. He called 911."

When King arrived on the scene, the neighbor met her and explained that the house was without electricity. The front door was unlocked, but King could not get it to open up very wide because something was blocking the door from behind. In order to get inside, King had to take off her gun belt and slide sideways through the crack. The neighbor was also slim, and he too managed to get into the house. Once inside the darkened home, King turned on her flashlight and realized why the front door would not open wider.

"It was like a scene right out of *The X Files*," she explains. "The living room was crammed full of garbage, and papers were stacked three-and-a-half feet deep right up to the front door. There was so much garbage piled around that we had to walk on top of it to cross the room. And there were cats *everywhere*, howling at us in the dark and jumping all over the place. I later counted twenty-seven cats in the house. The garbage was covered with cat feces, and it shifted around and sank as we walked on it and made our way across the room. The neighbor led me to a back bedroom where the woman was. Her body was cold. She had probably been there for days.

"I called the medical examiner. While I waited for him to arrive, two male officers came to help me, but they got so spooked that they left. Finally, the medical examiner showed by himself as he always does because they never have enough people, and I had to help him. We looked around and realized the only way we were getting her out was on a gurney through a bedroom window."

The medical examiner suggested King stay outside the window. He went inside, loaded the dead woman onto the gurney, and then started to push it and her out the window.

"I stood below the window as he started pushing the body through on the gurney," King says. "He had just wrapped a sheet around her before placing her on the gurney and, well, he didn't strap her down real well because as he passed her out to me the woman came off the gurney and landed right on top of me! I yelled up at the medical examiner, 'Hey, could you come out here and give me some assistance?!' And he did. We put her back on the gurney and he took her away. That was quite a night!"

Amazingly, some of King's DOA stories actually had happy endings. Her most successful case occurred when she was driving through a supermarket parking lot, and a store clerk waved her down to aid a man who had just had a heart attack.

"He was slumped over the wheel of his car, his eyes were open and fixed, and he was flat-lining," King recalls. "He had a very faint heart beat so I called in and requested a medic, then got into the trunk of my vehicle for the resuscitation mask only to learn parts were missing. Well, I threw that mask halfway across the parking lot because I was so pissed and my adrenalin was pumping. I pulled the man out of his car, threw him onto the ground, beat on his chest, and started giving him mouth-to-mouth for eight to ten minutes before the medics got there. It seemed like forever, and by the time they arrived I was just exhausted. What stuck in my mind the most was how hard it is to do mouth to mouth on somebody who's technically DOA. And because his eyes were open and fixed, all I saw were his blue eyes looking up at me. That really haunted me.

"I had no hope the man would survive," she continues, "but the medics arrived, put paddles to his chest, and then took him to a nearby hospital. As I stood up I was kind of hyperventilating, and I turned around and this lady said, 'I'm his wife.' She had been standing by the entire time I was trying to resuscitate him. I gave her a ride to the hospital. Later, I found out that he had made it. I was sent home early that day because I was just wiped out, and I remember going home and it was almost like I was floating five feet above the ground. It was really a bizarre thing. I was just emotionally toasted.

"The next day I went to the hospital to visit the man because I needed to see his eyes moving. His name was Mr. Crutchfield, and he was a little standoffish at first, as some people are after they've been through such a situation. But he got a lot better, he went home, and his wife called and asked me to come by and see him. We developed a friendship, and I would stop by all the time to see him. He was kind of a crusty, grouchy old guy, but he and his wife became like surrogate grandparents for me. And I ended up getting a bunch of awards from groups like the American Red Cross and the Seattle Heart Association. They couldn't believe that I had revived this guy. Nobody could because he was so bad off. But I just thumped on his chest and kept breathing into his mouth."

Several years later, King was working the same district and got dispatched to a barking dog call while another officer, also with the last name King, was dispatched to a DOA.

"It was in my area so I radioed that I would take it. But the other officer insisted that he had it covered. It worked out for the best because the DOA was this man, Mr. Crutchfield. The officer met with me later and explained. Mrs. Crutchfield was very relieved that it wasn't me because it would have been too hard for both of us.

"What's ironic," King concludes, "is that dealing with death and DOAs was something that I was most concerned about when I started as a police officer. Yet, if you look through my personnel file, probably eighty-five to ninety percent of my commendations throughout my career were for dead body calls and from families saying that I was sensitive. It got to the point where in the north precinct they used to call me the DOA Queen because I would no more than finish my lunch when I'd get a call on the radio, 'Uh, Nora 3, I hate to do this to you but...' 'I know, I have another DOA.' And off I'd go."

ON BEING GAY

Ever since the first female patrol officers were hired in the 1970s, they have had to confront a commonly held notion by many men that the only reason women become cops is that they are either looking for husbands, or they are lesbians.

"Early on in your career, you get a reputation," notes Sergeant Lis Eddy. "There were women who were known for sleeping around, and if you didn't then you were labeled a lesbian. I was clearly marked as a lesbian because I rode a motorcycle, I've always had short hair, and I didn't sleep around. I even had a female roommate who has been my friend since we were twelve years old, and we were just sharing a house because of expenses. All the signs were there. One guy even asked me, 'Hey, some of the guys were talking and they say women who come on the department are either looking for a husband or they're lesbians, and they want to know, which one are you?'

"I just looked at him and laughed. I said, 'Why does that have to be the case? Why can't we just be here because we want to do the job?'

"At first it kind of bothered me because I'm not gay," Eddy adds. "A lot of my best friends are, and I do kind of blend right in. I've been in women's sports all my life, and there are lots of lesbians in women's sports. It troubled me that people would be presuming something about me that isn't true, but then I realized I didn't care because I thought, *The only person who that should be important to is someone who's interesting in dating me.*"

For straight women like Eddy, earning such a reputation can sometimes be beneficial because it helps keep some of the *less desirable* male officers from hitting on them. But for women who are gay, being a minority within a minority can be very difficult and stressful.

"When I started on the Seattle Police Department back in the late seventies you had to be pretty closeted about things," explains Lieutenant Debie King, who is a lesbian. "You didn't want to be caught in a gay bar because back then the police thought nothing about walking in unannounced and messing with people. When some of the male officers learned that there were a few new female officers who were gay and frequented certain bars, there seemed to be a lot more bar checks. So it wasn't a real safe environment. I was too fearful to go into a bar, especially if there was no real good way out other than the front door because you didn't want to give them any more ammunition. They could surmise whatever they wanted, but if they ever caught you at a place like that, it would give a lot of credence to their little rumors.

"It was a real struggle, it really was," she adds. "You were kind of this two-sided person. You represented one person at work—the professional who aids people in crisis—and then when you were off work you were grappling with what it means to be gay."

While lesbians may have served on the department in the earliest days of the Women's Bureau, virtually all of the original policewomen were either married or widows, and American culture in the 1920s and 30s did not openly dwell on discussions of sexual orientation. And when the Seattle Police Department started hiring younger and mostly single females after the end of World War II, if there were suspicions about some of the women being lesbians, those rumors stayed largely in the closet.

"Back in the 1950s they indirectly asked about your sexual preference during the hiring process," recalls policewoman Helen Karas, who is heterosexual. "It wasn't put in those exact words. It was more like, 'Who are you dating? What does *he* do?' At the time I was seeing someone and they asked, 'Well, what does he think about you working for the police department? And where can we contact him?' It was all very sneaky."

In the aftermath of the Civil Rights movement in the 1960s, the topics of racism, sexism, and homophobia started to be discussed more openly in mainstream American culture. Yet, while the discussion became more open, so too did the prejudices around those issues. For female cops who were gay, the pressure became enormous.

"When I interviewed in the late 1970s, they asked about your orientation, only they didn't ask it that way," King explains. "It was the last and final question on the polygraph, and that was: 'Okay, we've talked about a lot of things today. We've talked about raising that shade on the window all the way up and revealing everything in the corners of the room. The last and final question is, Is there anything in your background or currently that would cause you embarrassment if it got out, that would maybe allow someone to blackmail you, have some sort of hold over you?'

"That question really pushed you into the corner of revealing your sexuality. And it scared the shit out of me because when they asked me that question in 1977, I had just recently figured out my orientation. It was very hard for me because I was still grappling with all of the issues. I sat there and, finally, I replied: 'Um, well, I think I am a lesbian.' "

To help her address all of the issues associated with her orientation, King went to a counselor for several years and learned how to tell her family and friends.

"However, even when I did come to terms with my orientation, I kept it to myself," she says. "Of course, that did not stop others from bringing the issue up. I got into a squad that had another female in it, and the guys were real protective of us. Well, one male officer who worked on a different squad began some rumors about myself and this other female, and they were very unkind rumors about our lifestyle. My lifestyle has always been my business and nobody else's. The rumors started getting out of control, and two guys in my squad took care of that guy. Let's put it this way, they did certain things to his locker, and then, when he didn't get the message, they had a discussion with him in the locker room. They wouldn't detail to me the total nature of the discussion, but the rumors stopped and the guy never made another peep.

"Being private about my private life, it bothered me that fellow officers were even talking about it. But what can a person do about that? You can't control your orientation any more than you can control what color you are. I don't like having my personal life talked about, but people talk about other people's personal lives all the time in this organization, as they do in other organizations. For my part, I never said yeah or nay, I never said anything about it."

Over time, as more women hired on to be patrol officers, the idea that some female cops might be lesbians became more of a positive than a negative.

"The guys got to the point where they really wanted to work with gay females," King notes with a laugh. "One, they thought we were tougher. And, two, we were no threat to their wives. So then they started trying to figure out who was and who wasn't, because if they worked with the gay female they could have the best of all worlds. For a while it seemed like the department was hiring a lot of gay women back to back, and the straight women who came on after us then suffered because the men started to think all the women coming on were gay. The women who weren't had to speak up and declare: 'I'm not gay!' Then, suddenly, we had two different groups of women, the ones who said, 'I'm not,' but they really were gay. And others who said, 'I'm not,' and they really weren't. I think some of those women felt compelled to prove they were straight by dating the male officers."

King says that initially she was concerned being gay would hinder her efforts to advance in the department, but she never found it to be an obstacle. In fact, she once refused a promotion when the Seattle City Council wanted to get a public relations boost by advertising her as a gay lieutenant. She eventually received her promotion, but without the lesbian-oriented fanfare. And, while King shied away from making her personal life public, she did later agree to serve a stint as executive director of Northwest Gay Officers Action League (NW GOAL).

"I went out and mingled with a lot of the private sector and sat on a lot of committees," she says. "I was not out or particularly open internally in the department, but externally I was. It was really interesting because all the people that I was around on the committees were very embracing and I felt very safe with them, safer than I do internally on the department. But then, they were all faced with the same issues in their organizations, so I guess misery loves company. And our Police Chief at that time, Norm Stamper, knew what I was doing and that didn't bother him. In fact, I frequently met him at community functions.

"But I had to be careful to make certain fellow officers and subordinates didn't perceive me to be agenda-driven," she adds. "If they saw me as being particularly geared towards gay or minority issues, then they'd see me the way I saw white males — that they're only interested in white male issues. So I really tried to appear neutral and open to everyone. That's how I've rationalized being gay and not waving a banner for it. But then, I looked around and I saw that nobody else was waving a banner either."

For some gay women on the department, their concerns about prejudice are compounded by other factors. For Detective Linda Lane, for instance, that would include being black and being female.

"There have been plenty of positions I've applied for," Lane explains, "that friends later told me I didn't get because I am black or I am a female or I am a lesbian. Sometimes it didn't have anything to do with being black. And sometimes, it didn't have anything to do with being a woman or black, it just had to do with being gay. Often times I didn't know if it was because I'm black, because I'm a lesbian, or because I'm Linda Lane."

"I've gotten to the point where I cannot figure it out completely because, especially since I was one of the founders of NW GOAL, my gayness became more of an issue. People reacted like, 'Well, you know, people guessed before, but nobody really knew. But now you're talking about it, bringing it all out in the open and causing more rifts and differentiations.' I responded by saying, 'I've never tried to use my gayness or tried to hide my gayness from anybody. And I've always done my work. Why should it matter? And why should I have to now figure out the political minefield of gender-race-sexual orientation? Why can't I just be the good cop that I've always been and have people accept me?' I saw other women who were straight who may or may not be of-color having to deal with gender bias, so maybe it's a no-win situation, no matter what you are."

Lane admits that figuring out the interplay between race, gender, and orientation can be very confusing.

"It's never clear-cut," she notes. "It really, honest to God, is not. If it were, I could deal with all of it a lot easier. Whatever new unit you go to, you have to try to feel your way through and pass all the tests about whether or not you're a good cop, you're brave enough, or tough enough to do all the things that they think you should be doing. All cops go through that. If you have a reputation that precedes you, good, bad, or indifferent, you still have to prove yourself, either to dispel a bad reputation, or to live up to a good one. Then, with some officers it's very clear that they don't like you because you're a woman. With others it's because you're black, or because you're a lesbian. With some it's all three. And then with some no matter what I did, or who I was, it would be okay.

"At one point in my career I really wanted to work Homicide, but I learned early on that it was a particularly male-identified unit, and while I am a good cop, I wasn't the right kind of woman that people want over there. According to one friend who worked in the unit, it all had to do with me being a lesbian.

She told me the men didn't want someone in the unit who was going to try to be more of a man than they were. I said, 'You're kidding. I'm trying to be a man?' And this person said, 'No, I know you're not, and a bunch of other people know you're not, but the people who are in charge don't feel comfortable with you.' So I asked about the other people who had applied for the position, and these other people happened to be white. A couple of them were lesbians too, but they were white. I was told they would be more acceptable to the powers in charge at that time than me. So there I got the indication that it was because of my race. But I still don't understand if that really was the issue. I think it could be a matter of personalities too. Perhaps I'm too independent and not subservient enough. I follow my orders and do what I'm told to do, but maybe I ask too many questions. Maybe I've put my nose into too many places. I don't know.

"There are definitely black males who do not care for lesbians, or for me in particular," Lane states in a matter-of-fact tone. "I could discover the cure for AIDS or for cancer and it would still be, 'Well, you know, she's something that's not right.' And there are women peers who have an opportunity to say something positive about me, but they choose not to."

Although Lane has been frustrated by such obstacles at work, her home life has been very fulfilling. She has been in a committed relationship for many years, and she and her partner have adopted two children, a little girl and a little boy. Having children has meant big changes in her life, and this has helped Lane put her professional life into perspective.

"I do think attitudes on the department about lesbians and gays are changing," she concludes. "But one of the first things you need to understand is that cops are different. Cops are real different. Most of us tend to be real rigid individuals, and change is hard. Human beings have a hard time with change anyway, but cops more so because change is something you can't control. And cops are used to being in control. But there are a lot of newer cops who are coming on, like me, who are helping to make change. It's gradual, it's painful, but it's coming."

For women who came on the department since the mid-nineties, the stigma of being gay has become less severe. Yet, challenges remain both on the department and out on the street.

"At work, I'm with the same people all the time," says Tracy Wood, who hired on in 1993. "There are people on the department who are ignorant and they continue to say ignorant things. I tolerate a lot of it and then choose my battles. One male officer who I now consider a friend thought it was absolutely disgusting that gay people have children, that gay people are in the military, and even that gay people are hired by the department. I explained to him, 'You have the right to do this; why shouldn't I have the same right?' I talked with him more and got to know why he thought the way he did. It was to do with his stereotypes about child molesters. I told him that it's usually straight people who do the molesting. Plus, just getting to know me and to realize that I'm not a freak also helped him. Some people have this perception that all gay people are bizarre. It sucks to have to explain how you're a person just like they are. But you have to do it and, hopefully, eventually they'll listen to you.

"I get called lots of names by the public too," she notes. "Dyke, bitch, cunt, this, that. Just nasty, nasty names. I just ignore them. I get called a dyke bitch all the time. Or they'll do it in front of other people like they're trying to 'out' me. If there are other people around, they'll say how I'm 'family.' Gay men especially have a big problem with lesbians. I don't know why that is, but they'll say things in front of your partner or other people about you being gay, or they will call you a dyke to try to upset you. It happens a lot, especially when we're down in the jail. Like, if somebody is mouthing off and I tell them to be quiet, they start into the dyke thing right away. 'Look at you with your short hair, you probably like women.' I say, 'Okay, you're right. So what?' It doesn't bother me.

"I think I've changed a lot of people's opinions because I'm really out, and I don't believe in not being out. I've been that way since the academy. I haven't had any problems except with individual people. It is really annoying to be the educator all the time, but I believe in the end you'll win out if you are patient. Instead of getting pissed off at people for being ignorant, you have to take the time to explain it to them. And you have to be willing to tolerate a lot of crap."

"When I first came on the department in 2006, the male officers did probably try to figure out my orientation," adds Officer Paige Maks, who is gay. "But I'm pretty friendly, and I'm pretty open. If a male officer hits on me, even in a joking way, I joke around with him and let him know he's not my type. I feel like the men I work with are comfortable around me and don't for the most part seem to have any issues with my being gay."

Before joining the Seattle Police Department at the age of thirty-seven, Maks was a lieutenant fire fighter on a rural department, and also worked in a lumber yard for many years. Both positions helped her make the transition to working on a police department.

"You have to prove yourself in any male-dominated work force," she explains. "Women are not completely accepted in the fire fighting world, and I really noticed that to be true also in the lumber yard. I drove a forklift, put together lumber packages, and loaded and unloaded trucks. To become accepted, I had to prove to the guys that I could do the job just as well as they could, or even better. Eventually, I became a supervisor, but when I started the only women they ever had working at the yard before me were the secretaries. Proving myself as a woman was much more of an issue than my orientation."

While it has become considerably easier to be out as a lesbian on the police department, this newfound freedom has created an interesting side effect.

"There are little societies of the women," explains one female officer who hired on in 2006, and requested anonymity because she fears being ostracized by other women on the department. "It's like in high school where there are definite cliques — groups of women who tend to exclusively talk to each other and spend time together. There are the sorority-looking straight girls who hang out with each other, and there are groups of lesbians from different generations. There are old-school lesbians who were straight until they were able to come out, and now they're hard core, and there are new-school lesbians who have always been able to be lesbians because they are younger and they came of age in a time when it's more accepted. Then there are floater lesbians, a few women who identify as being lesbians, but don't want to be a part of the lesbian cliques. They keep their private lives private, and just want to be known for being good cops.

"Of course, there are exceptions to everything I've said," the officer adds. "But, generally, if you threw all of the women into a room and watched who goes to which table, you would be able to categorize every table."

Despite the cliques, lesbians have slowly become accepted by the white male police establishment, just as they have in mainstream American society. But the change has come gradually and, of course, there continues to be prejudice against all minorities. While the vast majority of officers seem comfortable with their lesbian coworkers, the small number of intolerant officers continue to have their unfortunate impact.

"It's always about ten percent of the people who make minorities miserable," notes Assistant Chief Cindy Caldwell. "First, the white male officers picked on the black male officers when the department started hiring African American men. The old-time guys who came on in the sixties told me some horrible stories about the racism they experienced as the first black officers on the department. Then, when the women were hired for patrol, it was, 'Oh, well, at least the black officers are *men*,' and the men as a whole became more unified against the women. Then, when gay issues started to surface, the attitude about women changed to 'Oh, well, at least the straight women are good for something.' Now, the lesbians are more accepted and the gay men are on the spot. In the end, it's just basic prejudice."

9
HARASSMENT AND "THE CODE"

"There are three kinds of women who become police officers," says Suzanne Moore, a veteran detective who hired on with the Seattle Police Department in 1983. "The first kind is straight women who use all of their feminine traits and sexuality to play with the boys to get ahead. Some will actually say they came here looking for a husband.

"Then there are the gay women. One lesbian friend of mine says that if the men don't want to bed you, they simply ignore you."

"The third type is straight women who just want to do their job and go home. They don't try to fit in, and don't use their sexuality to play with the boys. But most of the men *expect* you to play with them, and if you don't—if you don't date them or go to coffee with them or sit around listening to them spout off about women—they take it personally. And they call you a *bitch*.

"In my twenty-three years on the department," Moore adds, "I have been groped, had my breasts discussed openly by officers in the precinct, and had a sergeant tell me, 'I can't have you work for me because if you did, all I would want to do is fuck you.' It has been pretty amazing. But you can't beef on the men because if you do it costs you huge. All you can do is keep your mouth shut."

Sexual harassment is not unique to the police profession. From 1997 to 2007, for example, the U.S. Equal Employment Opportunity Commission received more than 100,000 claims from women alleging workplace-related sexual harassment. In another study from 2006, nearly two-thirds of female college students surveyed in the U.S. reported experiencing some form of sexual harassment at their university, yet less than ten percent of these students told a university or college campus employee. Such statistics provide at best an indication of the problem, since it is impossible to know the number of cases that go unreported. Indeed, no one knows how many times women simply choose to *keep their mouths shut.*

Despite the prevalence of sexual harassment in our culture, female police officers admit to being shocked every time they personally experience or witness an act of harassment by one of their male colleagues. Perhaps it is the fact that officers are sworn to uphold the law, or it may be that female officers just can't believe their coworkers could be so insensitive. Either way, harassment is certainly not a new phenomenon.

"Clear back in the late seventies when the department really was full of good old boys, I witnessed a major do something awful to a lady civilian named Ilya," Assistant Chief Pat Lamphere recalls. "I didn't see *exactly* what he did, but I did see him bend over Ilya's desk, and then stand back up and walk away. I looked at Ilya and she looked shocked, and then I saw her get tears in her eyes. I walked up to her and said, 'Ilya, are you all right?' She asked if I'd seen what he did. I told her I did not. Then she told me—he had reached up the front of her skirt and went *tweak!*

"This guy was well known for being a womanizer," Lamphere continues, "and my husband was working traffic in his division. I don't know how the story got reported because you can believe I wasn't reporting it, and I don't think Ilya did. I don't know if she ended up crying somewhere and somebody else reported it or what, but supervisors came to me and asked me to give a statement. Normally, I am a pretty aggressive, don't-take-any-nonsense type of person, but when you're working within those systems there are some things you have to worry about. I was just a detective at this point, and I said, 'My husband works for him. Are you kidding?' They assured me that absolutely nothing bad would happen to us. With that assurance, I wrote a statement, and the major was forced to retire—something that was unheard of at that time."

While the civilian Ilya suffered a particularly shocking physical violation, sexual harassment can occur in a variety of ways, from verbal abuse to practical jokes and pranks that are designed to make women feel unaccepted. And, just as there are many different forms of harassment, there are also many different ways of handling it.

LETTING IT ROLL OFF YOUR BACK

"When I was brand new in patrol," says Lieutenant. Peggy Timm, "my sergeant would do things like, while we were standing around with a bunch of male officers, he'd say, 'Peggy turn around. We need to see something.' Well, what they were doing was checking out my body, and they were playing a little joke on me. I felt really stupid but, on the other hand, I smiled and laughed about it because they all liked me. They thought, *Yeah, she's fine, she's one of us. It's okay, we can tease her.* And they teased me about being short. It really didn't bother me that much because back then it just didn't. Nowadays, of course, it would, but when you're older you look back and you go, 'How did I let them get away with that?'

"There were several incidents of sexual harassment that happened to me, but I never did anything about them," she adds. "Lots of little things. One day I was walking in the police garage where all the police cars were kept. Every now and then, officers from other agencies would park in there as well. I was walking by officers from another agency who were bringing in some drunk guy in handcuffs, and one of the officers said, 'Don't you wish you had beavers like that working for you?' No one would ever say anything like that now, because the guy would be fired or he'd be demoted. Of course, back then I didn't talk to anybody about it. I just let it roll off my back."

For some women, the best way to deal with such instances of harassment is to just ignore them. They believe it is better to suck it up and let it go than to start an "incident" that results in an investigation. Other women see it differently.

"My preference was to always handle it directly," says Officer Mary Brick. "There was one officer who would routinely throw his arm around female officers and go kiss, kiss, kiss on their necks. One night I had just done an arrest. My hands were full carrying paperwork and he came up to me and kissed me on my neck. I backhanded him across the chest and said, 'Don't do that to me again.' Just at that moment a female lieutenant walked through the other door. She caught my eye and then she backed away. Later she called me into her office and asked me if I wanted to file a complaint. I said, 'No, absolutely not. If there are continued problems then maybe I'll come talk to you about it, but I just handled it.' And that was true.

"The male officer, who was a good friend of mine, didn't talk to me for about six months," Brick adds. "Finally, I went up to him and said, 'What's the deal? What's going on here?' He said, 'You really hurt my feelings. You know there was nothing personal about that. I do that to all the women.' I said, 'Yeah, that's right, but I don't like it and I told you so.' It had never dawned on him that maybe the other women didn't like it either. In fact a lot of women laughed when I told that story because it had happened to them too. He subsequently changed his ways."

"It is amazing to me," Lieutenant Joanne Hunt offers, "how many women are in this job where confrontation is something you do every single day, and they're afraid to be confrontational and solve these kinds of problems. Many women don't want to respond to some guy who's saying things to them, and they won't turn to him and say, 'Well, fuck you. Leave me alone.'

"When I was hired, I was older and I'd worked with men. That made it easier for me to deal with than someone younger who had never been subjected to that kind of male teasing. Male bonding sometimes does not appear on the outside to be much different than male fighting, with the kinds of insults and slaps on the back. If you're not used to that behavior, and if nobody has ever talked to you that way, then the first time somebody does it can be devastating. You just think, *My god, they hate me. They don't want me here. They think I'm awful.* That's not necessarily true. It may just be the way they tease. It's like little boys on the playground, or like when you were in second grade. 'Hey, you hit me! You must like me a lot.'

"There are some people who are going to probe to see if you've got a soft spot or if you're inclined to be vulnerable," Hunt continues. "But they do it to everybody. If it's something as simple as there's a nickname you hate being called, and you let somebody know you hate being called that name, rest assured that you will be called that name."

Both Hunt and Brick believe many incidents that are by today's standards considered harassment can be resolved if addressed quickly and directly. Even so, Brick remains surprised by the degree of animosity that continues to exist among some of the men.

"I don't think there should be a lot of differentiating between men and women and race and sex," Brick notes. "It should just be, Can you do the job? Of course, everybody does differentiate in our society, and in police work there is still a tension between the men and women. When I first came on, the tension was very open, very blatant, like the supervisor who said to me point blank, 'I don't think women belong in police work.' But today it has gone underground because it's not politically correct. A lot of the stories I've heard in the last five to seven years are scarier because they are more secretive, more underhanded, more emotionally damaging.

"Some of the women have had notes dropped in their lockers or pasted into their patrol cars that make references to words like 'pussy' and 'cunt.' Really horrible stuff. Whereas, when I was new and working with a male partner, members of our squad unbeknownst to us taped a 'Just Married' sign on the back of our squad car. It was all very out in the open.

"When I became a field training officer," she adds, "a lot of the new women were given to me for a night or a weekend so they could ask another female officer questions, voice their concerns and give feedback. I thought this was a great idea. Some of the women said their experiences were fine, but I had a couple of women burst into tears in my car. I remember one young woman told me her FTO baited her constantly. I knew enough about the individual she was talking about and had heard lots of stories about him, so I didn't discount what she said. I asked her, 'Why didn't you report it?' Her reaction was the reaction of most of the women and of some of the men who have found themselves in similar bad situations. She said, 'Who do you tell? You just want to become a police officer, and you know the training is going to be over in three or four weeks. So you just grit your teeth and bear it.' Her response was very common."

ROBOCOP

When pretty, blonde Suzanne Parton was finishing up her first year on the Seattle Police Department, she felt like she was finally settling comfortably into her life as a patrol cop. Not only was she learning to understand the unique rhythm of police work, but she was also enjoying a strong sense of camaraderie with her male coworkers. Then she had a shocking encounter with one male officer that changed her entire perspective.

"I call him 'Robocop,' " says Parton. "He was 6'4" tall, 280 pounds. He carried four guns at all times, one on his belt, one in his vest, one on his ankle and one in his back pocket. He was infamous for being 'the enforcer.' He was this big, strong, muscley, probably not-a-lot-of-brains sort of guy. He had saved somebody's life six months before when another officer got beat up by gangsters and had his gun taken away. Robocop saved the day so he was a hero. He was a man's man.

"One day I was eating my dinner and watching television in the lounge before my shift," she recalls. "My gun was in my locker. Robocop and another guy were there first, watching whatever it was they were watching. I didn't change the TV or anything—I didn't care. I was just sitting there eating my dinner. Then this segment came on the TV about breast cancer, and Robocop went off about women.

"He said, 'Their fucking tits! We're wasting our money on their fucking tits. They're not worth shit.' As he kept going off, it got worse. 'Men are dying all over the place of prostate cancer, and they waste all their damn money on women and their tits!'

"At this point, I was feeling uncomfortable," she continues. "We were in the lounge and I should have been able to eat my dinner there, but it was obvious he was having a bad day. I stood up. I wasn't positive I was going to leave, and I didn't need to confront him, but I wanted him to know I was there and that maybe he should be quiet. When I stood up, he turned to face me and went off some more.

"I decided to leave the room, but he stood in front of me and blocked my ability to get out. I was very intimidated because he was so much bigger than me and he had all those guns. I was thinking, *Maybe he's a little unstable the way he's going off.* Then he just finished with, 'Piss on women and their fucking tits!' And then he stepped aside.

"He did not touch me," Parton adds, "but he came just short of it. Then I got out of there. I needed to get some fresh air."

Once outside, Parton debated with herself. Should she report this or not? Ultimately, she decided she should.

"I knew the second watch lieutenant, and I was very comfortable with him," she explains. "I went into the lieutenant's office, but he wasn't there because he was on vacation. So I went to my own sergeant after roll call and told him what happened. He said, 'You realize now this is official, right? This is what you want to do?' I said, 'Yes.' He listened to everything, and that initiated my complaint. But it all went very, very badly."

Another male officer was present in the lounge at the time Robocop went on his tirade about women. Initially, that officer confirmed the incident happened as Parton reported. But later other people came forward who weren't present, and they made contrary statements that were accepted as fact. Parton's credibility started to crumble.

"And there was retaliation," she notes. "It was an awful experience. For over a year, I would walk into the lounge and the room would fall silent, and I might hear 'Bitch' or 'Cunt' under somebody's breath. During the investigation it was really bad. It was just an awful time for me. I remember I kept thinking, *Do I really want this job?* But I went through all that training at the academy, and it was such an accomplishment for me that I didn't want to give it up."

Ultimately, Parton's complaint was sustained, and Robocop received a letter in his file, a form of reprimand that seemed anti-climactic.

"At the time I thought, 'That's it?' But I was thankful too because I'd taken so much crap for just initiating the complaint. I had every right to file the complaint, and I would do it again. But if he had gotten into worse trouble, I would have been retaliated against even more. I'm sure of it.

"It was such a long road. I looked through my journal recently and came upon passages from that time. I wondered, *How did I get through it?* Even after all these years, I read the passages and I get mad. I'm glad it's over."

"I don't feel it really was sexual harassment," Parton concludes. "He probably chose me because I'm a woman, and he had issues with women. At the time I thought, *If he treats me this way, how does he treat women on the street?* But now I think if a small man was in the lounge instead of me, he might have been picked on. In the end, Robocop was just a jerk."

A TALE OF RACISM

Before she became a police officer, Tammy McClincy did not regularly think about her heritage as a Japanese American. In fact, during World War II her parents spent years in a Japanese American internment camp and, as a consequence, they raised her to downplay her race.

"When I was young I remember asking my mom one day, 'Are we white or black?' " notes McClincy, whose maiden name is Aoyama. "She said, 'Well if we had to choose we would be white.' As an adult I always think about that and wonder why she didn't say, 'You are neither white nor black, you're Asian.' But we never grew up thinking, *We're Asian American or Japanese American.* We grew up thinking we were just the same as everyone else."

However, when McClincy joined the Seattle Police Department in July 1985, she became the first Asian female officer on the department, and that made her different—whether she wanted to acknowledge it or not.

"On the last day of the academy, an Asian newspaper reporter came and wanted to interview me," she recalls. "I was thinking, *This is no big deal. Why are you making this a race issue? Just leave me alone.* It really wasn't something I thought about until the end of the academy when one of the instructors told me, 'Hey, you know, you're the first Asian female.' "

Once out of the academy, being Asian also made a difference to one of her field training officers, and he proceeded to put her through hell.

"I got my assignment, and one of my fellow academy mates called me on the phone and said, 'Hey I heard you're getting so-

and-so as your FTO. I just had him, and you are going to love him. He's great.' Then, later, the training officer called me and said, 'I understand that you've been told that I'm a nice guy. Well, I'm not.' At that point I didn't know what to expect, and I was a little scared. The next day I showed up at the precinct. He found me and introduced himself, and just the sight of him made me afraid.

"One of the first days we were together," McClincy continues, "we were on patrol. Out of the blue he asked, 'Were your parents in the concentration camps?' I looked at him and said, 'Sir, I don't know, I don't involve myself in that.' He ranted and raved about how wrong it was, and he used the word 'Japs' in the conversation. He had his flashlight out, and he was hitting the dashboard with it the whole time. I thought the best thing for me to do was to keep quiet and just let it go. And it passed.

"On one of my first calls with him we got sent to a car prowl on Beacon Hill. I looked at the victims' car, and then we went inside their apartment to take a report. They were Asian. As I was getting information from the victims, I grabbed my radio to get a case number and my radio wasn't working. So I said to my FTO, 'Can I use your radio?' He made some comment like, 'Well that's the problem you get when you use these Jap electronics.' The male victim looked at me like, *I don't believe he said that.* I didn't know what to do because I was a student officer, so I just kind of disregarded his comment. Nothing was ever said about it after that.

"Later I was driving on a particularly curvy road on the west side of Beacon Hill to get to the freeway. As I came around one of the curves, he said, 'Let's talk about the Domestic Violence Protection Act.' I said, 'Okay.' He turned to me and said, 'Let's suppose you and I are married and I punch you . . .' At that moment, while I was driving, he just wound up and punched me in the arm.

"The blow was so hard, it made me swerve the car sharply toward the edge of the roadway. I got control back of the car, but my whole arm was tingling. I looked at him like, *Don't you ever do that again.* But I didn't say anything. Then he said, 'Well, what if I hit you?' I replied, 'You'd be going to jail.' Back then I didn't know how to handle the situation. It was the most awful experience I've ever had. Just getting assaulted like that and thinking, *Can he do this to me? He's my training officer and I'm just a student, so I guess he can.*"

Back at the precinct, the officer sat McClincy down in roll call and told her: "I want you to know the Lieutenant and I are really tight, and all I have to do is tell him one word and you are gone. So don't you even think about telling anybody about any of this."

"I went home thinking he was going to get me fired," McClincy says, "and I was dreading going to work. On another day, I drove to work and didn't realize he was right behind me. When we arrived at the precinct, he got out of his car and started yelling at me about the way I was driving. That was a horrible experience."

Within a week of the assault, McClincy ran into one of her former FTOs who asked her how she was doing. She told him about a few of her experiences, and he encouraged her to report them. She said no. "I didn't want to stir up any trouble," she explained. But the former FTO acted on his own and reported the incidents to his sergeant, who subsequently told his lieutenant. The lieutenant called her, and ordered her to write a statement.

McClincy was promptly transferred to another field training officer. The offending officer retired not long after she filed her complaint, but the Equal Employment Opportunity ("EEO") unit conducted an investigation anyway. Two years later, the EEO came out with a report that effectively reached no conclusion.

"I get called into the EEO sergeant's office," McClincy explains. "I sat down and he said, 'You know, I'm done with this investigation, and basically the bottom line is that if we say we believe you, then that's the same as saying we don't believe what a veteran officer said. So, therefore, we believe him, and he said nothing happened.' I said, 'Okay.' I was in the office for maybe a minute or two, and that was the end of our discussion. The sergeant asked me to sign a form, and I did and I left."

To add a note of irony to her story, McClincy says the EEO sergeant was also an Asian American of Filipino decent.

"I was angry at the time," she notes, "but on the other hand, if the officer had gotten called for it, I would have been worse off. There's no telling what could have happened. During the investigation, I thought it was handled poorly. The EEO sergeant got a list of every student the officer ever trained, and he sent them this memo that said, 'Officer Aoyama alleges that Officer So-and-so did this and that. Did you ever experience any of that?' Because of the memo it became common knowledge around the department that I had turned him in, and I started hearing, 'What's wrong with you? What are you doing to him?' I just didn't want to deal with it. It was very traumatic.

"I've been through a lot on this department, and today if I saw somebody else being mistreated, I would be so angry I would say something because I wouldn't want anybody to go through that. But I never wanted to report my FTO because if you bad mouth somebody or turn them in, you will pay consequences for the rest of your career. A couple of years after this happened, a lieutenant I didn't even know came up to me in the West Precinct, and started talking to me about what happened. He told me, 'You don't need to turn in officers for that kind of behavior.' I had another officer, an Asian officer, come to me and say, 'You didn't need to do that to him. He was my FTO and he was great. You should have just taken it out back and duked it out.' To this day I get officers coming up to me and saying, 'Oh, you're the one who turned officer so-and-so in.' That officer is long gone, but I'm still paying consequences for reporting the incident.

"Since that time, I've been involved in other incidents that should have been reported," McClincy concludes, "but I didn't say anything because I've suffered enough. There was one incident I won't talk about because it was quietly dropped at my request. It was pretty serious stuff, but only a few people know about it. The guy eventually got transferred out of the precinct, but he went where he wanted to go so, ultimately, he was rewarded. But I can't complain because if I wanted something done, I could have stepped forward and said, 'Hey, wait a minute.' I didn't because of that one magic word: *consequences.* You pay consequences if you report it, and I do not want to pay that high a price again."

THE CODE

As Officer McClincy learned directly, if you rat on a fellow officer you pay a very steep price. To avoid such consequences, many officers remain silent when they suffer harassment, or they look the other way when it's happening to a colleague. They choose to honor "The Code of Silence." Long the favorite plot point of TV cop shows and legal dramas, the Code is in fact a compelling force on police departments across the nation. The Seattle Police Department is no exception, and many women cops have come to realize that if they break the silence, they will find themselves ridiculed and isolated.

"The Code of Silence is very real," says Marshal Rosa Melendez. "Law enforcement is still a male-dominated career, and the Code of Silence has not been beneficial to women nor to people of color. Women and people of color are the first ones sacrificed if that Code of Silence is broken. Those are the names that get dropped first. They're the ones who get blamed first."

The Code doesn't only apply to the victim officer. Supervisors also learn that witnessing an incident can open up a whole can of worms for them as well.

"I remember being in my second year on the department," Melendez notes. "I was assigned to the East Precinct, and the sergeant got up at the roll call podium and said, 'Ah, this is nothing. This is from the mayor. It's about sexual harassment.' It was a notice from the mayor's office saying that sexual harassment was against the law and the city would not tolerate it. The sergeant took the notice, folded it up and threw it into the garbage can. I thought, *Oh, hell, you just told me what's going to happen to complaints – they're going to be discarded in the garbage can.*

"I investigated those complaints as a sergeant and as an officer, and there was part of me that wanted to say, 'Don't say anything. You thought it was bad before? Wait until they find out you just filed a complaint.' And it always became true. Whatever the problem was before, the victim found it multiplied once it was reported. The male-dominated culture continued to blame the female, and that is still true. I'm talking about cases that involved legitimate complaints. Even as a supervisor, many times you did not even want to see an incident."

Harassment doesn't always take the form of physical violence, or even verbal abuse.

"I was in personnel when we investigated some gay-bashing incidents," Melendez explains. "It had just come out in the open that gays and lesbians were serving on the department. Some of the incidents were awful. Law enforcement is such a social environment in itself, and if you're not accepted in that environment, then you're just alone. So harassment doesn't have to be verbal or physical – sometimes it can just be isolation.

"One of the worst incidents I remember was one where a male officer committed suicide. Part of the problem was that people thought he was just too nice. He was not gay, but he was against police brutality and was a witness to several incidents involving a couple of gay officers. When internal affairs would investigate, he was always the first one to tell you what really happened. When you talk about that Code of Silence, well, obviously he broke the silence, and consequently he was isolated on the department. That isolation can be very difficult to live with, and I think that was one of the reasons he took his life.

"I remember another incident that involved a gay officer. We were in a meeting called on by the precinct captain, and the people in the meeting kept telling this officer that they would stand by him because they knew he wasn't gay. It wasn't until he said, 'But, I am gay,' that you saw repercussions that occurred to him after that— writing on the walls, the rumor mill. One thing you have to understand is that in a police department, if you are the victim of character assassination, officers are such a close-knit group that you're not going to be promoted; you're not going to go anywhere."

Melendez had personal experience with being labeled an outcast when she and a partner responded to a call involving three white men firing guns in the Central District, an area of Seattle with a large black population.

"As we were driving down Madison, we saw the suspects coming up Madison in a truck," she recalls. "As the truck drove up the street, somebody suddenly stuck a gun out of the vehicle and fired off a shot. Then I saw a black male on the nearby street corner falling to the ground, and I thought I had just witnessed a homicide. What really happened was that at the same time one of the men pulled out a gun to shoot off a round, the person on the street corner saw the gun and hit the ground. At the time he hit the ground, the gun went off and it looked like he had been shot.

"After we saw the shooting and the black male dropping, we made a U-turn and pulled the truck over. I was driving with a brand new recruit, and I told him, 'Pretend you're back at the academy doing a felony stop over the PA.' He understood, got on the PA and told the driver and passengers of the truck to step out with their hands up. At the same time, I jumped out of my patrol car with my gun drawn.

"The driver of the truck started to step out of the truck. As he did so he started to move his hands around his waist as if he was searching for something.

"I knew there was a gun in the car," she explains, "so I yelled at him to drop it. I kept yelling at him, but he continued to move his hands around his waist. I started pulling back on the trigger of my gun. I don't know how many people have told you, but when you're in that kind of a situation time all of a sudden slows down. So, as I pulled back on my trigger, the hammer started to draw back. I kept pulling back, getting ready to fire. I was just about to pull the trigger all of the way back when I suddenly heard an officer who was backing me up say, 'Oh, shit!'

"I thought, *Wait a minute. He said, 'Oh, shit,' and it was not like a this-is-serious 'Oh, shit.' It was more like, 'Oh, God, this is a fuck up of some sort.'* I thought, *This is not right for this scenario.* Then I heard him say, 'They're cops!'

Melendez immediately grabbed the hammer of her gun and threw herself down onto the ground.

"I remember to this day that all I thought in that moment of grabbing the hammer and putting my gun down to the ground was seeing the newspaper headline in the *Times*, 'Female officer shoots male officer.' In that instant, all I could see was the headline."

The three white males turned out to be drunk, off-duty cops, and when the driver emerged from the truck, he was fumbling for his badge. But Melendez couldn't see the badge. All she saw was the man fumbling around with something near his waist.

"I stopped myself from firing, and then everybody just kind of cleared out," she continues. "All the police cars that had come to back us left the scene. I walked up to the three off-duty officers and said, 'You assholes.' I realized who they were, and realized we were in the middle of a situation that could go really, really badly. I told them to just get out of here. I got back into my police car, and there were people standing around saying, 'If that had been us you wouldn't have released us,' and things like that. And they were right. I wouldn't have. If I had to do it all over again, I would not have released the officers."

The officers were sent home, but the matter did not end there.

"Our lieutenant called and said, 'Tell me what happened.' We went down to the precinct, told him what had happened, and identified the officers. The next thing I knew Internal Affairs was called in because by that time it had become a whole media event. It had become a race issue.

"It was one of those stories you never forget in your life. One of the things I tell officers now is, 'You and I can put in one hundred years of community service and spend hours educating the community, and one incident like that will destroy everything we've been working towards.' "

Melendez found herself under tremendous pressure from all sides—fellow officers who wanted her to stand up for her coworkers, and from citizens who were outraged because they thought she let the officers leave the scene. In subsequent hearings, she testified against her fellow officers and, ultimately, two of them were fired. Yet, while the officers clearly violated the law and department regulations, Melendez continued to experience cold shoulders from male officers on the department for many years afterwards.

"I reported one incident and the outcome was not good," recalls Detective Mary Ann Parker. "When I was on the anti-crime team at the East Precinct, I was the only woman on the five-person squad, and the only woman who had been there in a long time. There was one officer on the squad who thought I was liberal, and he made it his mission to poke at me about liberal things. He was about ten years younger than me, probably in his mid-twenties. I was doing some work up at Garfield High School trying to build relationships there between students and police, and he would make fun of that. He would say that I was up there trying to help misguided youth. He also used racial slurs while we were working with minority youths. He himself was a racial minority—he was Asian. But he liked to call blacks and gays really derogatory names. I complained because I got tried of hearing his comments all the time, but the supervisor never took official action. He too would hear the officer make racial comments, but all he would do was say, 'Don't talk like that.' "

Parker, who is white, also repeatedly told the officer she found his comments offensive and asked him to stop. The officer ignored her request, and continued to mock her.

"The situation came to a head when we worked a detail at Mount Zion Church for a Martin Luther King Day celebration," she explains. "I was assigned inside the church in plain clothes. At the end of the service, everybody joined hands and sang 'We Shall Overcome.' After we were done we went back to the precinct. At the precinct we had a raid board where you draw pictures and diagrams. He drew a picture of a stick person hanging from a gallows noose, and it said, 'We Shall Overcome' written over the top of it. It had my name written on the body of the person. He was laughing and making fun of it. The sergeant came up and erased it, and that was it. So I reported the incident to the lieutenant.

"The department handled it all wrong. I told them what had happened and asked to be transferred. They said, 'Oh no, you won't go anywhere; we're going to transfer him.' They then transferred him downstairs to the second watch in the same precinct, and left him right there. He goes downstairs and tells everybody that what happened wasn't true, and everybody felt bad for him because he'd been transferred out of the unit. Then I was looked at as this person who had ratted on somebody. It got all twisted around. He was so malicious that for years I had to ask the director of personnel to admonish him to stop being retaliatory. Nothing had ever been done about it, and everywhere he'd go he'd tell new people, 'Don't say anything in front of her because she'll beef you.' "

That was not the end of the story. The offending officer was eventually made into a FTO and was assigned student officers. One such rookie was a half-black, half-white man who looked Hispanic.

"This officer started talking in front of this student about zebra children and mixed kids. The student was an adult man with a family, and he filed an official complaint. Then the department pulled my situation into that allegation, and I had to go through this whole EEO investigation that I never initiated officially. The charge was sustained. The officer was disciplined and punished, and he got something like thirty days off. Then he had another complaint, and I think that also was sustained. But that happened right before he got *promoted*. One of his other punishments was he was on the sergeant's list when he got that first EEO complaint, and they didn't promote him at that time. He has allegedly now changed his ways because he wants to be a lieutenant.

"For a long time people would be afraid to say anything in front of me," Parker adds. "I was the victim, but I was labeled the villain too. That's why I say I would never do it again. I'd tell the person straight up to their face, 'Don't talk like that to me, about me, or in front of me.' And if they did it again, I'd just give them my own kind of discipline, like, *pow!* on the side of the head. That might sound violent but I think that may be the only way to get to their attention to make them stop.

"In the private sector, a person would have been fired right on the spot for drawing something like that on the board. They would be gone, their desk packed. But in the police department it's civil service. You have to show a pattern of behavior and an escalation of that behavior. No one-time thing. They wouldn't fire somebody over that. And though this officer had established a pattern of bad behavior, the department still didn't do anything. For me that was a bad experience, a very bad experience."

Parker remains hopeful despite her disappointment with how the department handled this officer.

"The Code of Silence has always been designed to keep everybody quiet," she says. "But I think in recent years this has changed, and making a complaint has become more accepted."

Indeed, over the past two decades, the Seattle Police Department has made efforts to address sexual harassment. In a groundbreaking study in 1992, eighty percent of female officers who responded to a survey said they had been victims of sexual harassment. Since that study, the department has continued to address sexual harassment claims as they come forward, and has tried to improve procedures to aid women who file reports. However, the actual number of sexual harassment incidents remains unknown because women still most often choose to keep silent.

"We really haven't come a long way in handling sexual harassment claims," notes Sergeant Lis Eddy. "If you have an incident with another officer, you have two choices: either you handle it yourself by trying to work it out with the other officer, or you tell your supervisor. If you do report it, your supervisor is then obligated to do something about it. If the incident is minor supervisors can handle it themselves, but most are afraid to do that. Instead, they hand it in to the EEO, and it becomes a full-blown investigation that usually gets very divisive and uncomfortable for all involved. So most victims won't make a report because they'll get dragged through the mill, and in most cases get treated like crap. I would never report an incident myself—I would just try to handle it on my own."

10

MIXED AFFIRMATION OF AFFIRMATIVE ACTION

"When I was five I told my dad I didn't want to grow up to have babies and be a housewife. I knew that would bore me to death. I wanted to be a career person. He said, 'Okay, this is what you're going to have to learn.' And so, that's where we went. He taught me how to be a good salesperson and how to deal with difficult people. He prepared me for everything except one thing: that I was going to be discriminated against when I got out into the work field. And, boy, did I. Before I joined the SPD I worked in sales, selling everything from chainsaws and tree trimmers to fine clothing. In that field I experienced a lot of discrimination and harassment, and one man even chased me around an office desk. Later I turned to my father and said, 'Dad, you forgot to tell me this.' He said, 'You know what? It never even dawned on me.' "
— Lieutenant Debie King

Affirmative action programs have been controversial since they were first enacted across the nation in the 1970s. Indeed, while virtually all of the women on the Seattle Police Department today benefited from hiring programs targeting females and minorities, they remain divided over the value of the boost and on whether some form of affirmative action is still necessary. And, from the very start, the policewomen of the Women's Bureau era were almost universally opposed to being given any advantage based on their gender.

"I would describe affirmative action as a necessary evil, but that was never the thrust of what we wanted," says policewoman

Beryl Thompson, who rose to the rank of Major. "We were never asking for special treatment. All we wanted was a foot in the door—the opportunity to take promotional exams, work in different positions, and prove ourselves. We weren't asking for any specific considerations based on being women. I think initially some of the women who came on in the late seventies and early eighties had some unrealistic expectations. I had the sense that they were looking at the job very differently and wanted too much too soon. Perhaps we didn't expect enough soon enough. We sort of sat back and let the movement start in New York and slowly move west."

"I am very much against affirmative action, selective certification, and the way the government handled it," Marshal Noreen Skagen adds. "When it was first suggested that women should be demanding the same promotional opportunities, the personnel department sent over a consultant who called a meeting for all twenty-one policewomen. We told her in no uncertain terms that we didn't want to be a part of affirmative action, that we trusted the department would do the right thing."

Looking back from an early twenty-first century perspective, it may seem odd that the policewomen were willing to trust the department, especially considering the white males who ran the Seattle Police Department had kept women segregated for more than fifty years. And it is more than a little ironic that some of the very policewomen who benefited from the end of segregation and the rise of affirmative action should be so against it. After all, without the national push for equality in the workplace, they might never have been allowed to advance.

"That's possible," responds policewoman Helen Karas. "I don't deny that at all. But we just happened to belong to the time that we did, and we grew up to take what was dished out."

"We figured we could campaign for ourselves," Skagen adds. "It was the department that commissioned the special committee at the end of the 1960s and accepted the committee's recommendation that women be dispersed throughout the department and be given the rank of police officer rather than policewomen.

"Since the department took that initiative, we figured opportunities were coming for us anyway. We felt that affirmative action appointments would result in a lot of suspicions, a lot of hostility, a lot of anxiety, and we didn't want it. We had worked with these men for many years. We respected them, they respected us, and we figured we could fight our own battles.

"But it didn't happen that way. It became a numbers game, and the first women who were promoted under affirmative action had a difficult time. We were dealing with a generation of men and women who weren't raised under these particular philosophies and ideals. There were morale problems and frustrations, and many relationships were damaged. Those were difficult years."

"I saw the need for affirmative action," counters Sergeant Karen Ejde, formerly of the Women's Bureau. "I didn't like it particularly because I felt there was a lot of unfairness, but I keep coming back to what Sgt. Elliott told me when I first started as a policewoman. She sat me down and said, 'No good thing is without its faults, and in terms of programs or methodologies, there are always going to be those who fall through the cracks, who misuse the system, or take advantage of it and make us all angry. You have to learn to live with them because you can help the majority.' I think a lot of people in my age category felt, yeah, maybe we didn't like affirmative action, but it was necessary to begin with."

"I think the department misused affirmative action," adds Sergeant Mary Robinson, also a former policewoman.

"Philosophically, I'm a supporter of it if it's done correctly because it is an opportunity to get more people, especially ones who had been overlooked in the past, into employment in areas where they weren't permitted before. But what I think the law said and what the practice has been is often very different. The law never has said people should be hired who are not qualified, but we saw that happen on the department, and I've seen it happen elsewhere in the city government. I think these problems come up because of how affirmative action has been administered, rather than the idea itself."

Just as the policewomen of the earlier era have differing opinions on the value of affirmative action, so do the women who most often benefited from it—female cops who were hired for patrol starting in the mid-1970s. For many, affirmative action was obviously a factor in their getting hired, but its ultimate value remains unclear.

"I think a lot of affirmative action is distasteful," notes Sergeant Cynthia Tallman, who joined in 1979. "But I truly believe that, unless forced, professions often don't open up to people who are different than those who are already in the profession. If you happen to have a group of all white males, they're going to be comfortable with white males. If you have two candidates of the same qualifications, or even if one is a little bit better, you're going to go to the person you're more comfortable with, and that's going to be another male. The same thing can be true if you had an all women-dominated profession. Your reference point always starts with who you are, and your comfort level often ends there as well. I think that sometimes without prodding, you aren't going to step out there and expand that comfort level.

"It has never been a completely fair playing field," she adds. "But in real life, is the playing field ever completely fair? In a big law firm, is the playing field any fairer for women? Probably not. I think you can make that characterization society-wide, except maybe in nursing and other fields where women dominate. I run into attitude dealing with a male auto mechanic when I'm trying to tell him what's wrong with my car. To him I'm just this woman who drives a car. That dynamic is going to exist no matter what you do. I think the department is taking steps to address as best they can the work environment issues, but the world is not perfect and I don't expect it will be in my time here. Affirmative action has been important because without it I don't think women would have been able to break in."

"In society, women are generally treated differently," agrees Officer Mary Ann Parker, who started at the Seattle Police Department in 1986. "As a woman I can't go into a parking lot when it is pitch black without looking around and peering into my car. But men can. I think we need affirmative action because I know there is still a lot of discrimination within units of the police department. I still hear people say things like, 'It's our unit, we'll decide who comes in here.' Or, 'We don't want her in here because she's a lesbian,' or 'We don't want him because he's black.' "

"One of the things that has *not* helped me is affirmative action," counters Sergeant Lis Eddy. "When I first made sergeant I was promoted right in order. In the past there have been a lot of out of order promotions, usually based on gender or race, people who have been down as far as 108th on the list. When I was promoted, the list I was on had about a hundred and twenty names on it, and I was sixth on the list. They didn't step over anyone to promote me. But many times I've been to meetings with men and I've felt I didn't get the credit for making sergeant on my own. I remember going to a railroad meeting when I was a First Watch supervisor. There were all these union railroad guys and as I walked into the room, you could just see it on their faces. You could watch their eyes go first to your face, then check out your size, your sergeant chevrons, and then they would look at each other and roll their eyes. I felt like saying, 'Excuse me, I scored a ninety-seven on the written test. I really do deserve to be here.'

"I was in another meeting about how to make the higher ranks more attractive, and there was some discussion about quotas. This one female captain said, 'Well, we have three female captains now. Do you think so-and-so has a chance of making captain since there are already three female captains?' I was struck by that comment. I thought, *What a thing to say*. It was sort of a slam to the individual, and it also was a way of saying, 'Well there are already three female captains so they're not going to let anyone else into the club.' My reaction was, Wait a minute. Why do you think that individual isn't smart enough to score number one on the test? She doesn't have to count on an affirmative action promotion if she's number one or two on the list."

"I think affirmative action is a slam against me," agrees Sergeant Carol Minakami. "You're basically telling me that I can't compete fairly, and that exceptions have to be made for me. My answer to that is that I can compete fairly, and if I want that job then I need to compete fairly.

"In the beginning there weren't a lot of women who got promoted fairly. It was all affirmative action, and it caused an extreme amount of resentment. You'd get a list of a hundred and fifty people and the white males were promoted right down the line, one two, three, four, then a woman at number eighty-five was promoted, then white male, six, seven, eight, nine, ten, then a black male at a hundred and five, then a white male, eleven, twelve. The people who ended up not getting promoted because they were stepped over for somebody way down the list had incredible resentment. We have fought that ever since. When you got it fair, you just wanted to say, 'I got it fair. I studied hard, and I got it fair.'

"I think you need to get minorities promoted, but to just make an exception and take people so far out of order, well, you're killing them," Minakami continues. "Who's going to respect them? You're not doing them a favor. If I, as a woman, know that the white males are being taken in order, and I score eighty-fifth on the test and take the promotion ahead of those ranked higher, how can I ever expect anybody to respect me? How can I ever expect to compete within this group of people? My answer is, let's find a way to bring these people up. Like with The Wall in the academy—if you want to get over the wall bad enough, you'll get over the wall. Physically, maybe people can argue that women are not equal to men, but mentally there is no reason why I can't compete fairly on a written test. For somebody to say, 'We need to make an exception for you,' is absolutely wrong. But that's basically what happened.

"I heard one black female officer say in the locker room, 'I'm a black woman, and they're going to promote me whether I score well on the test or not, so why should I study?' And she in fact did get promoted. That makes me wonder why should I try if they aren't setting any standards for me?

"I really believe that when you expect zero, you get zero. If you bring women and minorities into an all-white male world and say, 'Okay we're bringing these people in but we're going to make exceptions, we're going to take them out of order, we're going to pass others up, we're not going to expect the same thing from them as we do from white males,' you're creating division."

"I personally have never heard anyone make such a claim," responds Detective Linda Lane, an African American. "I find it very disconcerting that any minority, especially a female—whether black, white or whatever—would say something like that. When they do, they denigrate every single other person who has worked really hard to earn a promotion.

"I think affirmative action is still necessary. I don't like that it is, but there's still a predominant attitude of let me take care of my buddy before anyone else, and in most cases the buddy happens to be a white male. A lot of that is still going on. Affirmative action isn't the best of all systems, but why get rid of it and have nothing in its place? If they're going to get rid of it, put something better in place that's guaranteed to work or to at least try to work.

"I think a lot of people are comfortable with where they are and don't want to make waves," she suggests. "This can be said for affirmative action, too, with minorities not being supportive of affirmative action. They don't want to make waves, they don't want to be seen as a rabble-rouser or a troublemaker, and they're complacent with the way things are. Maybe they have achieved that queen bee or old-girl status. As long as they're seen as one of the good old girls and that helps them personally, they'll decide to forget about everybody else.

"Or maybe it's an attitude of, I can take care of everybody else once I get where I'm going. But until I'm where I'm going, I can't help you. Which is like, wait a minute! How did you get where you're going? If there hadn't been a Civil Rights movement, we wouldn't be here in the first place.

"I've heard some Latinos and Asians say they think blacks complain too much, and that attitude just kills me. I'm of the opinion that if Martin Luther King and other blacks hadn't complained and hadn't done all those things, blacks, Latinos, Asians, and women wouldn't have what they have now. There wouldn't be affirmative action period. If you're able to pass or pretend to be white and get what you want, that's all well and good. But if you're a person of color and you can't get what you need to survive, and you complain about it, especially if you're black, you're a whiner, a complainer, and a rabble-rouser. I don't think people know their history or care to learn about the history of the Civil Rights movement or of affirmative action. Even some younger people—black, Asian, Latino, whatever—look at it as the *past* and as something not pertinent to the present. They are wrong."

"Affirmative action helps women," contends Sergeant Frankie Burton-Barnet, who is also African American and joined the force in 1979. "Something that has always pissed me off about some of the white women who work here is that they are here because of affirmative action too, but they have this attitude that affirmative action is just for people of color. Oh, excuse me, sister, girlfriend. If it weren't for affirmative action, you wouldn't be here either. It helps all of us get our feet in the door. We have to do everything the men have to do to actually get the job, but it at least gets us a look."

Further confusing the debate is the fact that there have been many forms of affirmative action, and some have nothing to do with race or gender. After World War II, for example, G.I.s applying to police departments were given preference over non-military applicants. And, currently, when officers apply for promotions, they receive additional points based on the number of years they've served.

"On exams you get points for your written, points for your oral, and service points for how long you've been here," Burton-Barnet notes. "On one sergeants' list a white male officer and I had identical scores. But he had been on the department for a year longer than I had, and that put him forty people ahead of me on the list. Should the department give points for being here longer? When I was younger and hadn't been here very long, I said, 'No.' But now that I have seniority points myself, I'm less inclined to say that. So I'm still on the fence."

Women of all colors seem to have conflicting views of the ultimate value of affirmative action, and many can't escape the fact that, like it or not, they owe the start of their career to the breaks affirmative action offered.

"You know what affirmative action leads to?" asks Lieutenant Joanne Hunt, who is white. "It leads to people saying, 'I no longer have to be responsible for my own actions.' It leaves a large portion of the population believing that the only reason someone got promoted was because of affirmative action, and the person must be incompetent and not able to make it on his or her own. And people on the department do buy into that way of thinking. I know of one officer who, if she wasn't female, would have been booted out of her unit because, out of forty officers, she had the most complaints. Did they kick her out? No. They're afraid to reassign her because she said, 'They're doing this to me because I'm a woman.' Nobody sat her down and said, 'Bullshit!' A white male would have been out of there pronto."

"I have mixed feelings about affirmative action," admits Officer Mary Brick, who is also white. "It probably is what allowed me and a lot of women to get into fields we were interested in but were previously excluded. I remember back in high school I applied to get into the auto shop and drafting courses, and I was told I couldn't get in because only boys could take those classes. That was my first experience with that form of discrimination.

"Growing up I had never been told that I couldn't try something. Affirmative action probably did make it easier to get into police work. It's hard to know what the reality is. I mean, would I have been allowed to become a police officer if they had never laid eyes on me and just went by some set of test results? Would they have hired me or not? I don't know. I think affirmative action was good because it did open doors for women in a lot of different fields. But I don't think it's good to lower standards in order to get women and minorities into those fields.

"The issue of affirmative action came up for me years after I hired on when I applied for a position to teach at the academy. The sergeant interviewing me asked how I would feel about being called an affirmative action choice. I said, 'I don't care what they call me as long as I can do the job.' And I was fully qualified for the job, if not more than fully qualified.

"I like women, and I respect them and believe they can do whatever they want to do," Brick adds, "but I think they have to meet the requirements of the job. I hate seeing standards for hiring being lowered so that women or anybody can be allowed in. And the department has lowered the physical standards. They removed The Wall, and they have different standards for men and women for all kinds of things. But it shouldn't be an issue of men versus women. It should be a question of whether you have enough strength and capability to do the job. One of our routine calls involves lifting elderly people back into bed when they have fallen out and can't get themselves back in. We also have to deal with disturbances, have to jump over fences, and have to subdue people who are either really strong, on drugs, or strong and on drugs. Regardless of whether you're a woman or a man, you have to have enough strength."

"I don't know for a fact that affirmative action has directly affected me," says Officer Tammy McClincy, an Asian American. "I'm thankful that I have this job, but, on the other hand, I know I did well to get here. I know I'm qualified for this job, so I'm not here thinking, *Oh, I just got this job because I'm an Asian and a female and they're just carrying me because I'm both.* I think you shouldn't be here if you can't do the job no matter the color of your skin or gender. "

"I'm thankful for affirmative action because I think that's why I got hired so quickly," says Detective Jennifer McLean, who is white and joined in 1986. "It has opened opportunities up for me that might have not been there. Who's to say where the roadblocks would have been? I'm telling you that I haven't experienced the roadblocks, but had affirmative action not been in place, would I be sitting here saying the same thing? I don't know. That's what's so scary when they talk about taking it away. Do you think people automatically will say, 'Oh the world has changed now so we're just going to take the best person for the job, regardless of gender or race?'

"If they took affirmative action away, it wouldn't bother me one bit. But, again, I benefited from the system when I was hired on. I was qualified, and I got hired probably a lot quicker because they needed to fill some spots with women. That makes me think, *Am I closing the door to people by saying now it is okay to get rid of affirmative action?* They shouldn't lower the standards for any unit. For instance, if you can't ride a bike, you shouldn't be on the motorcycle squad. But if they didn't have affirmative action, would people even get a chance? Had affirmative action not been in place, would Carol Minakami have ever been allowed in SWAT? I don't think so.

"I got put on the Anti-Crime Team, where we do all the search warrants, and I don't know if I would have been put on there as quickly, or at all, had they not needed to have a woman on the team to show good faith that they were doing things for women. I just don't know. I don't have a lot of trust there yet. Without affirmative action, I'm not sure people would get the chance to take the test, whatever the test is. They wouldn't get their foot in the door.

"Seattle is a different climate, maybe more liberal, so maybe it wouldn't be as bad. But what about other places around America and other police establishments? I've had friends who work for smaller departments where, if affirmative action hadn't been there, they'd be gone. There would be no opportunity for them."

"I am totally pro affirmative action," notes Marshal Rosa Melendez. "I was an affirmative action hire, and all my promotions were affirmative action. I scored high on the list but they still had to skip a few to get to me. It's always been hard from the standpoint that I always felt that I had to show that I deserved it, and I was qualified. But I think one of the things affirmative action appointees feel is that they have to be better. You almost become a perfectionist, and it's very difficult because none of us are perfect. You try not to make any mistakes because with the first mistake you make, you're going to hear, 'Well, see!'

"I am on an advisory committee for the National Center of Women and Policing, and one of the things I've discovered is that once the court orders have been stricken or the injunctions have ended, the hiring of women decreases dramatically. We had one surge where a lot of women being hired, and now we're at a point where the hiring of women has reached a plateau and is in decline. Affirmative action is still necessary."

Despite the progress and the ongoing debate among the women about the value of affirmative action, gender-induced tensions remain even in 2008, making it difficult for some women to discuss these issues openly.

"I'm concerned about speaking on the record because I joined the department in 2006, and my career is just starting," explains one female officer who asked to not be identified by name. "I love being a police officer, and I enjoy working with my male counterparts. But I think a lot of the male officers would be put off if they heard a woman being candid about some of the issues, and I would be ostracized. Some of the other women who have been interviewed for this book, like Suzanne Parton and Sergeant Lis Eddy, have all been on the department for a long time, and their careers are established. But I'm in my infancy and everything you do affects your career.

"I would say the general consensus in the women's locker room is that our gender affects our job," she adds. "You'll hear a lot of talk that people are watching us more, taking note if we are surprisingly successful or if we are tripping up along the way. If twenty-five people are qualifying at firearms, twenty-four of whom are guys and only one is a woman, everyone will know how the woman did. They are looking to see how she scored. Or, if there was a scuffle with suspects the question is always, 'Did she get into the fight?'

"When I was getting hired on I was initially more concerned about my gender on the streets, about how I would handle being in a fight with a man who's stronger than I am. But I came to realize it's really more about your gender on the department and the dynamics with your coworkers than it is about being on the street. Men pay attention to how many relationships a woman has had, who she's dated, who she's been with, and if she's with a man or woman. There have been guys who talk of having sex with thirty chicks, and that does get highlighted, but it's never seen in a negative light. There are some women who are great detectives or police officers, but when their names are mentioned, the first thing people talk about is who they're dating, or how many men they've supposedly slept with. What does that have to do with police work?"

Despite the tension over gender, this female officer opposes affirmative action and does not believe it is necessary.

"We are afforded certain opportunities just because of our gender," the officer observes. "If they need women to buy narcotics or do vice stings, we get additional experience and overtime, where a rookie male officer might not. And when we lost a female assistant chief, we got another female assistant chief. Is that just about filling a spot? I don't know. I don't want to be commenting on chief of staff, but I would never want to be a quota. I want to be selected for my strengths and for what I have to offer.

"I don't believe I was hired based on affirmative action, and I don't believe affirmative action is necessary. I'm strictly talking about gender. Certainly, the department should be targeting women and minorities in their recruiting efforts so the department better reflects the community at large. But when it comes to the actual hiring process itself, they should hire the best candidates. I don't know if they were looking for a certain number of female officers when I was hired, but there were a lot of women testing at that time, and I would like to think I was hired because I was the best candidate."

From a twenty-first-century perspective, the affirmative action programs instituted in the 1970s and '80s may appear to be oddly contrived and unnecessary. Indeed, they may even seem like artifacts from the past since most, if not all, of the programs have been slowly phased out in the last twenty years due to citizen-sponsored referendums, adverse appellate court rulings, and changes in legislation. As a result of this phase out, police departments like the Seattle Police Department no longer use any form of quota system, and women are seemingly hired alongside men based solely on their merits.

This might indicate a victory for true equality. However, many of the departments that hired female officers when affirmative action was in place did so only after their local courts ordered them to, and the result was more women in uniform. With the end of these formalized hiring programs, the percentage of women on police departments nationwide has declined significantly. This drop may be due a variety of factors, including better job opportunities in other industries, and changes in attitudes about the desirability of police work. Either way, there are fewer female officers on the streets today, suggesting the debate over the value of affirmative action is far from over.

11
WILL THE NUMBERS EVER BE EQUAL?

"John Wayne never had a woman standing at his side as an equal. The whole mythology of our country has been that the man is the strong one— the man is the head of the household. Do you know what characterizes this still? Religion. As long as theology continues to put men and women into these gender roles, we will always have a lack of equality."
—U.S. Marshal Rosa Melendez

"New female officers today still face challenges because the dynamic between men and women in our society has not changed all that much. We thought we would see a difference with the men who grew up with their mothers working. We thought they would see women differently. But that has not really happened. This is true not just in police work. Women face this working as stock traders on Wall Street and in many other male-dominated professions. It's our culture. There are still so many men out there who are threatened by women."
—Lieutenant Debie King

In the one hundred years since women were first hired to serve on police departments nationwide, they have made tremendous progress in establishing a foothold in what was once exclusively a man's world. Female officers have broken out of the segregated Women's Bureaus, have earned the opportunity to compete head-to-head with their male counterparts, and are routinely seen walking the beat on American streets. Yet, as the centennial anniversary of the first policewoman approaches, one question remains: Will the numbers ever be equal?

In April 2002, the National Center for Women and Policing released a study summarizing the status of female officers in police departments across the country. Titled *Equality Denied,* the report concluded that "despite overwhelming evidence that women and men are equally capable of police work," females accounted for only 11.2 percent of all sworn law enforcement personnel in the United States. By comparison, fifteen percent of the American armed forces are women, and females make up 46.5 percent of the overall American work force. The study identified a variety of reasons for the low percentage, from widespread bias in police hiring, selection practices, and recruitment policies, to the end of formal affirmative-action type programs.

In Seattle, after initial success recruiting women in the 1970s and '80s, the Seattle Police Department found its percentage of female officers dropping in the early 1990s to less than ten percent. In comparison with other major departments in the country at that time, Seattle ranked ninth overall behind cities like Pittsburgh (24 percent), Memphis (15.8 percent) and Portland (12.7 percent). Eager to understand why the Seattle Police Department was losing women, the Seattle City Council pressed for an investigation. Pat Lamphere, who had risen up the chain of command from a Women's Bureau policewoman to the rank of Assistant Chief, was given the task of supervising a year-long study. She surveyed women across the department, and conducted one-on-one interviews to better understand the issues they faced.

"I learned a lot from doing the study," Assistant Chief Lamphere says. "First, I realized that many of the issues women raised related more to being new cops rather than being women.

They were expecting things they shouldn't have right away, like the respect of their fellow officers or the ability to work in different units on the department. What they wanted to have right now, no new young white male is going to get either. You have to pay your dues to the system before things start clicking for you. I was really surprised that so many women took some of the issues personally. They thought it was because they were women, and I thought it was because they were new to the job.

"One issue that did directly affect the women was the lack of childcare. It's a problem for men too, but not to the extent it is for women because everybody still thinks of women as the primary caregivers. We met with city officials about the issue, but our local government could not come up with twenty-four-hour daycare because it was too costly.

"During that year-long study, I also discovered that I became far more supportive of women's issues than I had ever been before," she adds. "I started realizing that women needed to be more supportive of each other in order to surmount some of the difficulties that came from working in a man's world. I retired from the Seattle Police Department in 1993, and sometime just before that I had an informal get-together for policewomen. I did it because I'd learned that women needed more networking with other women. We must have had sixty women attend. I met officers I had never known before, and they were able to converse informally with women of all ranks. It seemed to be very successful, but nobody ever followed up by organizing another gathering."

In the early 2000s, the Seattle Police Department directed Sergeant Lis Eddy and two other female officers to do a follow-up study to better understand why women leave police work.

"We talked to women who had left the department, to women who were thinking about leaving, and to women who had no plan to leave," Eddy recalls. "The common answers revolved around the family and daycare. A lot of women who had left said they would come back part-time if that were allowed. Their decision to leave had to do with the shift work. A lot of them said 'I wanted to start a family and be a full-time mom.' You can't argue that."

As a result of that survey, the Seattle Police Department developed a program that allows male and female patrol officers to serve part-time so that they can take time off to have children or to go back to school. The program has proven to be popular, and may in part account for the fact that the percentage of sworn female officers on the Seattle Police Department has grown to 14.5 percent.

However, while there are more women on the department than there were ten years ago, representation at the higher ranks has thinned dramatically. In 1997, there were eight women holding the ranks of lieutenant, captain, or assistant chief. In addition, three out of the four precincts in Seattle were supervised by female captains, and the North Precinct had both a female captain and a female lieutenant in command. In 2008, by contrast, there was one assistant chief, no captains, only three lieutenants, and none of the precincts were headed by women.

"We lost a lot of high-ranking women in a short period of time," explains Lieutenant Debie King. "I've tried to get female sergeants to take the lieutenant test, but they don't want to be lieutenants. The lieutenant's job is pretty tough because you're caught right in the middle between the officers and sergeants who work the streets, and the upper management that sets policy. You face a lot of no-win situations. A lot of sergeants—male and female—don't want the job, so it's been hard to get more women to move up the chain of command."

Regardless of the reasons for the lack of high-ranking women on the department, the question remains: why are the overall numbers of women in police work still so low?

"When I was a background detective working in personnel with the recruiters, I could see a couple of reasons why Seattle has a difficult time hiring African American women," offers

Sergeant Frankie Burton-Barnet, who is black. "First, the African American population in this area of the country is not very large, so there just aren't as many people to draw from. Second, a lot of the black women I talked to were not interested in police work. They wouldn't mind working for the police department, but they don't want to be a police officer. The law enforcement part doesn't seem to appeal to Asian and Latino women either. Some of them say, 'Well, I wouldn't mind being a detective.' I tell them, 'You're thinking *Cagney & Lacey*, and it's not like that.' Caucasian women have a whole different attitude about it, and I don't know where that comes from. Perhaps television. *Cagney & Lacey* and *Charlie's Angels*—they're all white. Maybe they watch those shows and think, *I can do that*."

"A lot of women come into this job with a perception of police work that differs from the reality," says Lieutenant Joanne Hunt. "They don't realize what a paramilitary organization is like or how a chain of command really works. And this job is twenty-four hours a day, seven days a week. Somebody has to work from eleven at night to seven in the morning. Somebody has to work Saturdays, Sundays, Thanksgiving, Christmas. I don't know how much you can do to alleviate that. I don't think the solution is to let only women get Christmas off, or let only the single parent have weekends off. If you're a single parent and you're in a unit that gets called up, what do you do with your four-year-old at two o'clock in the morning if you don't have a spouse that's home?

"The minute there is a child involved in a police officer's life, the job becomes immensely more difficult and less desirable. So some women get disillusioned a little faster. And there is a lot of competition for jobs. Everybody is trying to hire females and minorities. If a woman gets a better offer from someone else—a job where they can make as much with the same benefits, work from seven till three in the afternoon and have weekends, nights, and holidays off—they're going to go take that offer.

"Probably the biggest problem with the job is that we *see* too much," she adds. "We see a lot of ugliness. Take something like a hideous murder in a neighborhood. Immediately following the murder, counselors arrive to counsel people who never saw anything, but live nearby and are traumatized by the fact that this happened in their neighborhood. They didn't see the bodies, they didn't see or smell the scene, they didn't have to handle the aftermath. But everybody knows that they're traumatized. And, yet, they assume that I, as a police officer, shouldn't be, that I should be able to look at such ugliness day after day after day and just go merrily on my way. I don't like seeing this stuff any better than anyone else does. Some people—male and female alike—just don't want to see that much."

"Day in and day out I battle with whether or not I want to be a police officer," says Detective Jennifer McLean. "The other people in my family have normal jobs, and they don't go home with a lot of emotional baggage from what they've seen during their day. I struggle because of the stress of the job, the cynical way of looking at people, and the awful things I see. And, as cops in Seattle, we get abused. We're one of the most professional departments in the country, but we have citizens who will say the most awful things about us and to us. We get verbally abused, we get physically assaulted, and we get reamed by the press all the time.

"Everybody loves a fireman, but nobody likes the police, and it is really hard to always have that negativity coming at you all the time. I like to have a good outlook towards life, and I don't think all people are bad. I think the press has a lot to do with the negativity. Maybe you were at the scene of an incident or know what happened, and then you see something completely different on the news. It's hard not to listen to it. We have to absorb the after effects of that coverage, and nobody comes back and says they're sorry to us afterwards when the story gets corrected—if it gets corrected. That's when I think, *Gee, why don't I go work for Microsoft or do some job like that?*

"Some days the public's reaction to you is good, and some days it's bad," notes Officer Paige Maks, who joined the Seattle Police Department in 2006. "Some days they hate you, some days they thank you. Some people are very grateful, some people can't stand you. I love being a police officer because the job is different every day and I love helping people. But it's hard sometimes because there are times I don't know what the public want me to do? You get mixed messages. You see things where people say, 'Why are you harassing that guy on the corner for no reason?' Well, I'm not harassing him for *no* reason. I saw him do something illegal.

"Then, on the other hand, you have people saying, 'Why don't you do something to the drug dealer standing on the corner? Can't you see what they're doing?' Where I work, I generally feel the community as a whole appreciates us, but we do get mixed messages, and that can be very frustrating for some officers."

Ultimately, the reason for the disparity between males and females may simply be that most women do not want to do police work.

"It doesn't matter that our numbers aren't equal," says Sergeant Eddy. "You have to look at the nature of the work. Police work is not the type of job that attracts everyone. If you polled a bunch of civilian women on the street and asked them if they wanted to be police officers, my guess is that about fifteen percent would say yes. So I think that number is reflective of the interest in the job. And when you talk with women cops, I don't think they care that the percentage is low. They think, 'It's okay—*we're* here.' "

"I don't think we'll ever be beyond twenty to twenty-five percent, and that's perfectly acceptable," adds Assistant Chief Lamphere. "There are certain jobs the majority of women will never want to do. It's just like there are jobs that men don't want to do. The key is giving women a chance to do the job. The opportunity needs to be there."

"Regardless of the percentages, we've proven the point," Eddy concludes. "Women have shown that they bring a lot of strength to this kind of work, and I don't think you can say this is a job for one gender or the other. The best response by a police team at an incident is a mixed response where both male and female officers are involved. The fears about women cops that existed in the early days have dissipated. Certainly, there remain issues that need to be addressed between men and women, just as there are in everyday life, but I believe the police community and our society at large have come to accept women as police officers."

The year 2010 marks the one hundredth anniversary of the first policewoman and of the first time a female was allowed into the all-male world of police work. As we move into the next century, women will continue to create their own unique definition of what it means to be officers, and to be the commanders of officers. Challenges still remain—from sexual harassment and low representation, to the seemingly still-present glass ceiling. As the struggle for complete equality rages on, women will continue every day to prove they do indeed represent a different shade of blue, and police work will be the better for them.

ACKNOWLEDGEMENTS

There are many people to thank for *A Different Shade of Blue: How Women Changed the Face of Police Work*. First, I am very grateful to the policewomen and female officers who agreed to go on the record and share their experiences. I offer special thanks to Norma Wilson, Jean Selvidge Dunbar, Karen Ejde, and Helen Karas for providing me with many newspaper clippings, photos and other background materials that were invaluable in preparing this book. Regrettably, Helen passed away on October 30, 2006, at the age of eighty-six. She was "one tough broad," and a true delight.

In addition to the women who appear in the book, I would like to thank Carmen Best, Kim Franklin, Ann Martin, Joy Munde, Deborah Nicholson, Linda Pierce, Erin Rodriguez, Diane Stone-Wherley, Yvonne Underwood, Susan Vijaro, and Barbara Wilson for graciously granting me interviews and for sharing their insights.

I must also thank the inimitable Ann Rule—former policewoman, now best-selling author—for writing her lovely foreword, and for her kind support over the years.

I received encouragement and support from many other officers and civilians at the Seattle Police Department. In particular, special thanks to goes to Mike Germann, Pat Howard, and Assistant Chief Jim Pugel. Also, I am grateful to the Seattle Police Department Officer James Ritter, who in his spare time manages the Seattle Metropolitan Police Museum, and to his assistant at the museum, Judy Thomas.

On the photographic front, I must thank my dear friend Paul Verba for the author's photo that graces the back cover. Special thanks goes to Judy DeMillo and Dave Storm at the SPD for granting me access to the Seattle Police Department photo archives, and to Mark Mann of the Washington State Criminal Justice Training Center for allowing me to reproduce police academy photos. Panda Photographic Lab in Seattle made all of my digital and film copies, and did a fine job.

Among my many supportive friends, I wish to single out Deborah Horne, who helped edit early versions of the manuscript, and who convinced me to stop rewriting endlessly and to start looking for an agent. I also owe thanks to Rick Shenkman, a fellow writer who provided many valuable insights into the publishing world; and to Dan Gallery, who designed a thrilling website to promote my book.

Thanks also go to Kimberly Mills, a wonderful editor at *The Seattle Post-Intelligencer* newspaper. Over the years, Kimberly has published several articles of mine, including a version of *Blue's* Chapter Five that was timed to the 25th anniversary of The First Nine hitting the streets. Her support and encouragement helped convince me to pursue a full-length book.

The Behler Publications team was amazing. Lynn Price, my publisher, was simply terrific—always on call to calm this nervous writer's anxieties. Editor Erin Stalcup was a dream to work with, and a great partner in the editing process. Erin's keen insights immensely improved the manuscript. My thanks also to Cathy Scott for creating the cover design.

Lastly, I must say "Thank you" at least *one million* times to my agent, the extraordinary Janet Reid. To say she was tireless in her support of *A Different Shade of Blue* would be an understatement. Finding the right publisher can be more difficult than dating, yet she persevered and found the perfect one for my book. Janet, you are simply way too hip for this planet!

NOTES & SOURCES

Please note: Many of the women interviewed have since changed their last names due to marriages and divorces, and their ranks may have also changed. In *A Different Shade of Blue*, their names appear as they were when they were interviewed, but their ranks have been updated whenever possible. The author apologizes for any inadvertent errors that may have occurred.

Preface:

Lis Eddy was interviewed on May 16, 1997; July 15, 1997; and July 9, 2008.

Chapter One—In the Days of Soiled Doves and Lily Wavers:

Norma Wilson was interviewed on February 6, 1999.

Jean Selvidge Dunbar was interviewed on August 21, 1999.

Seattle history from the early 20th century is documented in *HistoryLink's Seattle & King County Timeline*, written by Walt Crowley and the staff at HistoryLink, University of Washington Press, 2001, 92 pp., pages 21, 49, 53.

The quote explaining the duties of the early policewomen as the "wearing of the 'star' and the authority to make arrests, just the same as any blue coat on the force," is from *The Seattle Post-Intelligencer*, July 11, 1912, pg. 4, col. 5. This quote and other details in the same paragraph were drawn from the research done by Policewoman Nancy Robert Post, for her 1953 master's thesis, *A Description and Analysis of the Duties Performed by the Staff of the Juvenile Bureau For Girls of the Seattle Police Department*. A copy of the thesis was provided to the author by Policewoman Norma Wilson.

The quotes by Mrs. Sylvia Hunsicker appeared in a newspaper clipping from a Seattle newspaper. The clipping is unidentified, and came from the personal collection of Policewoman Helen Karas.

Additional information about the early years of Seattle policewomen was found in *A History of Policewomen in Seattle*, a research paper written by John C. Hampton, Jr., University of Washington Society & Justice 400, August 6, 1973, 25 pp. Copy on file at the University of Washington Allen Library.

Chapter Two — Social Work With a Gun and a Badge:

Karen Ejde was interviewed on October 28, 1998; December 19, 1998; January 16, 1999; and August 15, 1999.

Helen Karas was interviewed on October 28, 1998; December 19, 1998; January 16, 1999; and August 15, 1999. Helen passed away on October 30, 2006, at the age of eighty-six.

Mary Robinson was interviewed on August 5, 1999.

Beryl Thompson was interviewed on November 19, 1997.

Noreen Skagen was interviewed on October 27, 1997.

The duties of Seattle policewomen were detailed by Policewoman Nancy Robert Post in her 1953 thesis, *A Description and Analysis of the Duties Performed by the Staff of the Juvenile Bureau For Girls of the Seattle Police Department*. She submitted the thesis in support of her Masters of Social Work from the University of Washington. The author received a copy of Policewoman Post's thesis from Norma Wilson.

Jean Selvidge Dunbar provided additional information about Captain Irene Durham in her article, "Founder Pioneered in Police Service," which appeared in *Landmarks: Magazine of Northwest History and Preservation*, Vol. 3, No. 3, 1984.

Another source for information about Captain Irene Durham is Lucille MacDonald's article, "Seattle Policewoman Has Watched Crime Change in 30 Years," *The Seattle Times*, Sunday, August 26, 1956, pg. 8.

Chapter Three — Noses Powdered and Ready for Duty:

Pat Lamphere was interviewed on October 10, 1998.

Marlynn McLaughlin was interviewed on October 14, 1997.

The quote that opens the chapter, and the quotes by patrol division Chief Charles A. Rouse, come from *The Seattle Times* article written by Barney Harvey, March 23, 1961.

Chapter Four — Upwardly Mobile... At Last:

Details about the New York City lawsuit can be found in Dorothy Moses Schulz's book, *From Social Worker to Crimefighter: Women in United States Municipal Policing*, Praeger Publishers, 1995, pp. 125-28.

The final report by the International Association of Chiefs of Police was issued in June 1968 under the title *A Survey of the Police Department, Seattle, Washington*.

The quotes by Assistant Chief Richard G. Schoener appeared in *The Seattle Post-Intelligencer* article, "City Policewomen Take Giant Step — In Patrol Car," written by George Foster, May 23, 1973.

Chapter Five — The First Nine:

A version of this chapter first appeared in *The Seattle Post-Intelligencer*, under the title "The First Nine — Lure of Equal Pay Changed the SPD Culture Forever," Focus Section, October 28, 2001, pg. D4 (D Section of The *Sunday Seattle Times*). Republished on the web at HistoryLink.Org under the title, "Seattle's First Female Officers on the Beat: Seattle Women in Blue."

Joanne Hunt was interviewed on October 27, 1998.

Teri MacMillan was interviewed on September 8, 1997.

Leslie Baranzini was interviewed on February 13, 2000.

Vicky Burt was interviewed on March 14, 2000.

Debbie Allen was interviewed on July 17, 1997; January 7, 1999; and December 26, 2000.

Marsha Camp was interviewed on August 6, 1997; and December 14, 2000.

Mary Kulgren was interviewed on July 31, 1999; and December 17, 2000.

Peggy Timm was interviewed on October 18, 1999.

Chapter Six—The Next Wave:

Linda Lane was interviewed on September 10 and 17, 1998.

Rosa Melendez was interviewed on October 15, 1998.

Cindy Caldwell was interviewed on July 8, 1997; and November 17, 1998.

Toni Malliet was interviewed on August 14, 1997.

Daljit "Dolly" Gill was interviewed on July 22, 2008.

Linda Patrick was interviewed on June 26, 1997.

Wanda Barkley was interviewed on July 10, 1997.

Mary Ann Parker was interviewed on November 19, 1998.

Mary Brick was interviewed on October 31, 1998.

Carol Minakami was interviewed on August 25, 1997.

The shooting of Officer Nick Davis was covered extensively by the Seattle newspapers. In addition to the comments by Detective Linda Lane, the author relied on articles in *The Seattle Post-Intelligencer*, written by Michael A. Barber, December 19-24, 1984.

Chapter Seven—Fitting In:

Tammy McClincy was interviewed on November 11, 1999.

Megan Bruneau was interviewed on July 16, 2008.

Jennifer McLean was interviewed on September 3, 1998.

Debie King was interviewed on December 22, 1998; January 6, 1999; and July 31, 2008.

Chapter Eight—Survival Strategies:

Irene Lau was interviewed on July 12, 1997.

Tracy Wood was interviewed on June 23, 1997.

Chapter Nine — Harassment and "The Code:"

Suzanne Parton was interviewed on May 14, 1997.

Suzanne Moore was interviewed on April 3, 2006.

The U.S. Equal Employment Opportunity Commission (EEOC) maintains statistics on charges filed. For more information see http://www.eeoc.gov/stats/harass.html.

Statistics on sexual harassment on college campuses can be found at American Association of University Women website: http://www.aauw.org/research/dtl.cfm. The statistics used in this chapter were drawn from the AAUW study by Catherine Hill and Elena Silva entitled, *Drawing the Line: Sexual Harassment on Campus*, which can be found at:

http://www.aauw.org/research/upload/DTLFinal.pdf.

Chapter Ten — Mixed Affirmation for Affirmative Action:

Cynthia Tallman was interviewed on December 2, 1998.

Frankie Burton-Barnet was interviewed on January 27, 1999.

The early history of affirmative action programs is discussed in Kerry Segrave's *Policewomen: A History*, (McFarland: 1995) pp. 124-27.

The impact of removing affirmative action requirements is explained in the report, *Equality Denied: The Status of Women in Policing: 2001*, National Center for Women & Policing, April 2002, pp. 11-12.

http://www.womeninpolicing.org/PDF/2002_Status_Report.pdf.

Chapter Eleven — Will the Numbers Ever Be Equal?:

Paige Maks was interviewed on July 25, 2008.

For complete statistics on the status of female officers in police departments across the country please see: *Equality Denied: The Status of Women in Policing: 2001*, National Center for Women & Policing, April 2002. The report can be found at: http://www.womeninpolicing.org/PDF/2002_Status_Report.pdf

The percentage of members of the armed forces who were women, as of September 30, 2004, was obtained from *U.S. Census Bureau Press Release: Facts for Features*, February 22, 2006 (citing *Statistical Abstract of the United States: 2006, Table 501*). http://www.census.gov/Press-Release/www/releases/ archives/facts_for_features.

The 1992 survey of female Seattle police officers is presented in the report, *Council Work Program Request Retention of Women Officers*, by Assistant Chief P.A. Lamphere, Public Safety Committee Meeting, May 13, 1993.

Additional Bibliography

Abrecht, Mary Ellen with Barbara Lang Stern, *The Making of a Woman Cop*, William Morrow, 1976.

Appier, Janis, *Policing Women: The Sexual Politics of Law Enforcement and the LAPD*, Temple University Press, 1998.

Fletcher, Connie, *Breaking & Entering: Women Cops Talk About Life in the Ultimate Men's Club*, Harper Collins, 1995.

Gallo, Gina, *Armed and Dangerous: Memoirs of a Chicago Policewoman*, Forge: 2001.

Harrington, Penny E., *Triumph of Spirit: An Autobiography by Chief Penny Harrington*, Brittany Publications:,1999.

Hays, Gayleen, *Policewoman One: My Twenty Years on the LAPD*, Villard, 1992.

Myers, Gloria E., *A Municipal Mother*, Oregon State University Press, 1995.

Schulz, Dorothy Moses, *From Social Worker to Crimefighter*, Praeger, 1995.

Segrave, Kerry, *Policewomen: A History*, McFarland, 1995.

Taubman, Byrna, *Lady Cop: True Stories of Policewomen in America's Toughest City*, Warner Books, 1988.